Tracking the Great Bear

The Nature | History | Society series is devoted to the publication of high-quality scholarship in environmental history and allied fields. Its broad compass is signalled by its title: nature because it takes the natural world seriously; history because it aims to foster work that has temporal depth; and society because its essential concern is with the interface between nature and society, broadly conceived. The series is avowedly interdisciplinary and is open to the work of anthropologists, ecologists, historians, geographers, literary scholars, political scientists, sociologists, and others whose interests resonate with its mandate. It offers a timely outlet for lively, innovative, and well-written work on the interaction of people and nature through time in North America.

General Editor: Graeme Wynn, University of British Columbia

A list of titles in the series appears at the end of the book.

NATURE | HISTORY | SOCIETY

Tracking the Great Bear

How Environmentalists Recreated British Columbia's Coastal Rainforest

JUSTIN PAGE

FOREWORD BY GRAEME WYNN

UBC Press • Vancouver • Toronto

22 21 20 19 18 17 16 15 14   5 4 3 2 1

Printed in Canada on FSC-certified ancient-forest-free paper
(100% post-consumer recycled) that is processed chlorine- and acid-free.

Library and Archives Canada Cataloguing in Publication

Page, Justin, 1973-, author
    Tracking the great bear: how environmentalists recreated British Columbia's coastal rainforest / Justin Page; foreword by Graeme Wynn.

(Nature, history, society)
Includes bibliographical references and index.
Issued in print and electronic formats.
ISBN 978-0-7748-2671-6 (bound). – ISBN 978-0-7748-2672-3 (pbk.).
ISBN 978-0-7748-2673-0 (pdf). – ISBN 978-0-7748-2674-7 (epub)

    1. Environmental protection – British Columbia – Great Bear Rainforest.
2. Environmentalism – British Columbia – Great Bear Rainforest. 3. Environment-alists – British Columbia – Great Bear Rainforest. 4. Natural resources – Social aspects – British Columbia – Great Bear Rainforest. 5. Natural resources – British Columbia – Great Bear Rainforest – Management. 6. Sustainable development – British Columbia – Great Bear Rainforest. 7. Great Bear Rainforest (B.C.) – Environmental conditions. 8. Actor-network theory. I. Title. II. Series: Nature, history, society

TD171.5.C32B75 2014   333.7209711'1   C2014-901960-2
                                                            C2014-901961-0

Canadä

UBC Press gratefully acknowledges the financial support for our publishing program of the Government of Canada (through the Canada Book Fund), the Canada Council for the Arts, and the British Columbia Arts Council.

This book has been published with the help of a grant from the Canadian Federation for the Humanities and Social Sciences, through the Awards to Scholarly Publications Program, using funds provided by the Social Sciences and Humanities Research Council of Canada, and with the help of the University of British Columbia through the K.D. Srivastava Fund.

UBC Press
The University of British Columbia
2029 West Mall
Vancouver, BC V6T 1Z2
www.ubcpress.ca

For Elika

May you one day set foot in the Great Bear Rainforest
and there experience one good, common world.

Contents

Rethinking Environmentalism

Graeme Wynn

There are at least two good reasons to read this book. The first is for the story at its centre – the remarkable re-conceptualization of British Columbia's mid- and north-coast timber supply areas as the Great Bear Rainforest. The complex, multifaceted, and momentous set of developments that brought this about are summarized here to provide context for, and perspective on, the second valuable contribution of this book – Justin Page's careful explication of his particular approach to telling this story. Woven together as they are through the pages that follow, the tale and Page's reflexive telling of it are reasons enough to find in this slim volume an invitation to think anew about the shape, form, and tactics of environmental activism and about human-environment relations.

Amid the groaning bookshelves and general clutter in my academic office, a large poster covers part of a room divider. It is no triumph of artistic design. The photograph that provides the background of the poster is striking. Taken in the Yakoun Valley of Haida Gwaii, it is all massive, gnarled Western Hemlock trunks with bright green ferns in the understory. But less than a third of this scene is visible, as text boxes and other images are superimposed upon it. Three photographs define a strong vertical axis in the upper centre of the poster. The topmost is an aerial view of the heavily forested Quaal River valley in Douglas Channel, near Kitimat; the lowest shows a "sub-adult" grizzly bear; and the centrepiece is a picture taken in the middle of a clearcut in the Natlamen watershed of Haida Gwaii. In the upper right quadrant of the poster are three maps showing the original North American distribution of coastal temperate rainforest, the extent of coastal rainforest in British Columbia in 1845, and the much-reduced reach of that forest in 1995. Balancing this on the left is a block of text, much of it in a small and nondescript font, detailing the provenance of the maps, pointing out that over 20 percent of the world's remaining temperate rainforests are in British Columbia, and informing readers that "this highly productive, severely threatened forest supports one of the most abundant fisheries on earth" and "provides a critical refuge for grizzly bears, salmon, and a rare white version of the black bear." All of this is drawn together, in a messaging if not an artistic sense, by a phrase prominently emblazoned across the poster, somewhere above its vertical midpoint: "ENDANGERED RAINFOREST." Beneath this is another, larger insert – a map of the BC coast and islands stretching from just south of Port Hardy to just north of Prince Rupert. This identifies the "Top 10 Threatened Areas" between Knight Inlet and northwestern Haida Gwaii under the title: "ON THE CHOPPING BLOCK – SOON TO BE LOST TO CLEARCUTTING AND ROADBUILDING."

Produced in the mid-1990s by BC Wild for the Canadian Rainforest Network, this poster took its place with a series of somewhat similar creations intended to rally support for the defence of wild places in British Columbia against the ravages of commercial exploitation. It appeared when the summer of protest in Clayoquot Sound, the pivotal episode pitting environmental protesters against logging operators in what came to be known as the "War in the Woods," was still fresh in peoples' minds. Between May and August 1993 well over ten thousand people had spent time at the protest camp set up alongside the highway to Tofino, and almost a thousand were arrested for blockading access to logging operations. Things were quieter the following year, but protest still simmered.[1]

This particular poster may be somewhat less captivating, aesthetically, than most of its earlier counterparts, but it surely sparked memories in the minds of British Columbians and others who looked at it in the mid-1990s. The "Endangered Rainforest" prompted recollection of countless images in pamphlets and flyers, the pictures in newspaper advertisements, the strikingly beautiful full-scale posters, and even the magnificent coffee table books produced in the previous decade or so in support of campaigns to save the Stein, the Carmanah, and the Walbran Valleys, and to expose people to the splendour of Meares Island, Clayoquot Sound, and Lyell Island.[2] The call to ban clearcut logging of old-growth forests across Canada, issued from the epicentre of the Clayoquot protest, had reverberated across the country, and the poster's visual declaration that endangered rainforest was on the chopping block echoed a familiar, confrontational refrain.

Yet the discourse of environmentalism was changing, even as the poster identified the ten most threatened sections of forest on the central coast. In the long economic boom that ran from the end of the Second World War into the 1970s, British Columbia's coastal forest industry prospered through the implementation of what some have described as the Fordist compact. This was an implicit agreement reached by corporate interests, organized labour, and the state to improve the efficiency of production, ensure good wages, and sustain the industry by the legislative sanction of logging operations and the implementation of a range of fiscal and social welfare policies.³ With strong and stable markets for construction-grade lumber generated by the North American housing boom, large capital-intensive operations harvested the rich temperate rainforests on government-granted tenures to feed giant mills that produced a markedly homogeneous set of products. The pace of the onslaught was fierce, increasingly mechanized clearcutting was standard practice, and residents of single-industry towns prospered. At the same time, logging's impact on the landscape grew ever more obvious, and wilderness lovers and others appalled at the devastation before them rose to mount a series of campaigns to protect particular locations from despoliation. The stakes were serious for all sides, but this was in some sense a game – a competitive activity with certain rules – that was a distraction for the companies (which by and large believed that there would always be new valleys to log) and a determined pursuit for activists who reveled in victories won and girded loins for battles to come.

In the 1980s, however, the British Columbia forest industry (and with it the economy and the political administration of the province) faced a number of serious challenges. Old mills were less efficient than new-built counterparts elsewhere, especially as computer-controlled and highly mechanized milling operations became the norm. The Stockholm Conference of 1972 had heightened civil society concerns about environmental devastation and spawned and invigorated a number of environmental non-governmental organizations that raised public concern about logging practices in British Columbia. Opposition to imports of Canadian wood from the US lumber industry challenged the stumpage system governing access to the BC forest, led to the imposition of countervailing duties, and undercut established markets. Declining global markets and increasing competition from producers elsewhere also challenged the profitability of the BC industry. At the same time, increasingly forceful, and compelling, claims to rights in and title over their traditional territories by First Nations groups in the province disrupted established assumptions about the very bedrock of the industry, its access to timber.⁴

Then, the protests at Clayoquot Sound sent strong shockwaves through the already crumbling foundations of the postwar consensus.[5] Facing a looming economic crisis in the forest industry as well as seemingly worldwide disdain for allowing logging to proceed as it had, and acutely conscious of the potentially devastating effect that international market boycotts of the sort pioneered in the Clayoquot campaign could have upon the sale of BC wood products, the provincial government acted quickly. In 1994 an "Interim Measures Agreement" was signed with several First Nations of Clayoquot Sound, recognizing the responsibility of hereditary chiefs to conserve and protect their traditional lands and waters for generations to come. Meanwhile a newly minted Commission on Resources and Environment sought (with limited success) to bring stakeholders to negotiated agreements on regional and local resource-use goals in four areas of the province where these issues were particularly contentious. In 1994, CORE released its recommendations for a provincial land-use strategy, and the next year the government introduced a highly prescriptive Forest Practices Code to increase environmental protection and establish a consistent set of rules for forest licensees.[6]

These highly visible actions were strategies intended to secure the future. So too – although far less noticed at the time – was a parallel initiative aimed at securing the forest industry's wood supply. Between the inception of protests against logging in Clayoquot Sound and the government's acceptance of the sweeping recommendations of a scientific panel on the area in 1995 (limiting clearcuts to four hectares, reducing the annual allowable cut, and establishing a moratorium on logging until the completion of a detailed inventory of pristine areas), the industry had increased its interest and operations in the mainland's Mid-Coast Timber Supply Area. Conscious of the particular conjuncture of circumstances that had escalated the Clayoqout protests to global visibility and forced government and industry to react, the newly re-elected administration in Victoria sought to get out in front of developments and establish a collaborative process to steer development on the mid-coast. In 1996 they initiated a Central Coast Land and Resource Management Planning (CCLRMP) process. By inviting representatives of local communities, leaders of companies that were interested in exploiting the resources of the coast, union representatives, members of interested First Nations and ENGOs, and other stakeholders to the table, they aimed to forge consensus around a plan to protect some 2 to 3 percent of the area from exploitation.

This prospect pleased neither First Nations nor ENGOs. First Nations agreed to join the deliberations, but only as observers, insisting that the

CCLRMP process had no authority to make decisions about territories to which indigenous people had claim, and adamant that they were not just one among several stakeholders with an interest in the region. Scornful of the tiny fraction of the area to be protected and afraid of being co-opted by participation in a government–led process, ENGOs turned their backs. In the summer of 1995, a coalition of environmental groups – the Raincoast Conservation Society, the Sierra Club of BC, BC Wild, and the Valhalla Wilderness Society – had initiated efforts to set aside Princess Royal Island and adjacent parts of the mainland coast as a sanctuary (somewhat akin to that established in 1994 at Khutzeymateen for grizzly bear protection) for the Kermode bear (a cream- or white-coated variant of the black bear). According to environmental activist Tzeporah Berman, Greenpeace members had also begun to strategize about the mid-coast a year before the CCLRMP process began, after a meeting with Peter McAllister, founder of the Raincoast Conservation Society, and his son Ian. By Berman's account, the McAllisters pointed out that only 69 of some 360 rainforest valleys along this stretch of the mainland remained undisturbed, and stressed the futility of campaigning to save one or another of the pristine areas (Johnson Valley? King Island?), while other parts of the coast were devastated.[7] Instead they argued for a concerted campaign to protect the entire area.

New knowledge of this relatively inaccessible territory had become available in the previous five years. In 1991 the Earthlife Canada Foundation and Ecotrust/Conservation International published an inventory of watersheds in coastal British Columbia by forester and geographer Keith Moore and Spencer Beebe, the founder of Portland-based Ecotrust.[8] Using air-photos, satellite imagery, and BC Ministry of Forests logging data, Moore offered an important synoptic view of the region, indicating that two-thirds of coastal valleys had been significantly affected by industrial development, that another sixth had been modified to some degree, and that barely a fifth remained pristine. Four years later, the first publication of newly established Ecotrust Canada – an offshoot of the Portland organization – was a "bioregional portrait" that presented information on forest cover and indigenous languages as proxies for the larger issues of forest integrity and cultural diversity in coastal temperate rain forest areas between California and Alaska.[9] The maps in this "Atlas of People and Place" spoke volumes, and their message was summarized in the accompanying text. "The south-to-north advance of development and indigenous cultural loss in the North American coastal temperate rain forest" was "abundantly clear." South of the 49th parallel "biological and indigenous cultural integrity" had been greatly diminished, "at a price reckoned not in dollars but in human communities, living species, natural processes, and knowledge of the ecosystem." Better stewardship was needed, urgently. Protecting "natural areas and cultural traditions" was essential to recovering what Oregon writer Kim Stafford "called 'the nourishing ways': the local knowledge that quietly affirms 'this is how to live in this place. In this way, it becomes our home.'"[10]

Eight million hectares of coastal temperate rainforest – the "last remnant" of its kind – running back from a spectacular island-and-inlet studded coast to clothe mountain slopes with one of "the most complex and diverse ecosystems on Earth"; a rare sub-species, revered by First Nations as the spirit bear, with broader "charismatic megafauna" potential; a strong First Nations presence in the area and the corollary expectation that they were anxious to protect their territory; the call to affirm the value of intimate familiarity with nature; a strong sense that the CCLRMP process was but another manifestation of the "talk and log'" strategy attributed to corporate and government interests through the preceding years; and a fear that the Forest Practices Code would disperse logging activity and lead companies "to invade remaining coastal watersheds at an accelerated pace" – all of these things were siren calls to environmentalists.[11]

Some environmental groups were quick to adopt familiar forms of direct action. In September 1995 the Forest Action Network (FAN), a grassroots organization with an office in Bella Coola, joined the Nuxalk First Nation in a blockade of logging on King Island. Shortly after a dozen or so environmental groups came together as the Coastal Rainforest Network in June 1996, Greenpeace called for a ban on logging in British Columbia's old growth forests. In 1997 there were more blockades on King and Roderick Islands. But the central coast was not Clayoquot Sound. Because it was accessible only by sea and air it was difficult to muster large groups of protesters; a few activists might chain themselves to machinery, but it was a sizeable challenge to get news coverage of such actions. Moreover, relations between First Nations and environmentalists were far from easy. Many members of the small indigenous communities on the coast had come to rely on income generated by the forest industries. As much as they deplored the devastation of their traditional territories, they needed work and were acutely aware of the alignment of interests between the provincial government and logging companies. So a majority of Nuxalk voted to ban FAN members from their reserve and, despite an earlier understanding between them, the Kitasoo First Nation denounced Tzeporah Berman and Greenpeace as eco-imperialists.[12] Protests mounted in a spirit of common cause were denounced for dividing indigenous communities. Solidarity was usurped by acrimony and distrust, and provincial government representatives publicly chastised Greenpeace for following "the route of conflict and confrontation." Forests Minister Dave Zirnhelt made his government's position clear – the Roderick Island protesters, he said, "are breaking the law and their activities are not welcome – not by Western Forest products, not by the Kitasoo First Nation and not by British Columbians" – but Premier Glen Clark was more direct in concluding that "environmentalists who ... work with American interests against our industry and jobs are enemies of British Columbia."[13]

Thwarted in their attempts to develop traction by bringing people to the forest, environmentalists redoubled their efforts to "bring the forest to the people" by developing slide shows and other materials to support a market campaign against the products of BC's three largest logging companies, all of whom had operations on the mainland coast that contributed, Greenpeace said, to the felling of "an acre of rainforest every sixty seconds" in the province.[14] Re-envisioning the coast as the Great Bear Rainforest (a coinage invented by Peter McAllister in 1993 or thereabouts) was central to the success of this strategy. The iconic, somewhat tantalizing, name that respected the presence of First Nations people by avoiding the designation "wilderness," and gave space for concern about the habitat of both Kermode and grizzly bears, quickly became a powerful symbol of place, and invited people to think again about human-nature interactions. Faced with rising consumer resistance to the sale of products made of "old growth" forests, major home-improvement retailers, including Home Depot, Lowes, and Menards, refused to buy wood from "environmentally sensitive areas." A parallel campaign in Europe led the German Publishing Association and the Belgium Paper Association to cancel contracts with companies logging Canadian rainforest. By most accounts, these developments cost the BC forest industry tens, even hundreds of millions of dollars in lost contracts.[15]

Logging companies soon responded. One divested its cutting rights on the mid-coast, one adopted variable retention logging in place of clearcutting, and another offered a moratorium on logging in certain areas while the CCLRMP process unfolded. The locus of power had shifted, and it had done so remarkably quickly.[16] As Merran Smith of ForestEthics and Art Sterritt of Coastal First Nations reflected in their joint telling of the Great Bear Rainforest story, in 1996 "power was firmly in the hands of the BC government, which owned the land; and the forest companies, which held the rights to log and manage much of the region's forests."[17] However, by the end of the century, market campaigns had so emphatically increased the heft of the environmental lobby that it could no longer be marginalized as a temporary irritant. During the same period, First Nations groups that had largely acted independently of each other came together with impetus from the David Suzuki Foundation (and in light of Ecotrust Canada's insistence that this "spectacularly wild" territory was properly considered the Great *People* Rainforest) to form Coastal First Nations, a coast-wide alliance to implement ecologically, socially, and economically sustainable forms of resource management on the central and north coasts and Haida Gwaii.[18]

Recognizing that the game had changed, several forest company executives and their advisors from Canadian Forest Products, Catalyst Paper, International Forest Products, and Western Forest Products met in 1999 to find ways of reducing conflict over coastal logging. It was soon apparent that the industry needed to change its relationship with environmental groups; that the interests of First Nations, local communities, and other stakeholders had to be heeded; and that new forms of forest management attentive to a wide range of forest values were necessary. In this new order of things, environmental stewardship was recognized as a core social value and negotiation was seen to offer the best route forward.

As the CCLRMP process bogged down, representatives of half a dozen major forest companies and four leading environmental groups sat down together in January 2000 as the Coast Forest Conservation Initiative. Intent on finding a long-term solution to the mid-coast/Great Bear Rainforest conundrum, their first step was to declare a moratorium – an eighteen-month period during which logging would cease across a considerable part of the coast and the market campaign against wood from the rainforest would be curtailed. Promising as this seemed, the CFCI soon began to splinter. Some companies lost access to much larger areas of forest than did others. The provincial government was not happy at the subversion of its own process. Neither First Nations nor union representatives were part of the initiative, and other groups were suspicious of the CFCI's agenda; indeed the Truck Loggers Association characterized it as nothing more than "an ill-advised effort to placate some large environmental groups."[19]

Forced to take a step back, members of the CFCI were encouraged to develop – with First Nations and other interests and in liaison with the CCLRMP – an "ecosystem-based model for conservation and management of coastal forests" that fully integrated social, ecological, and economic needs. Only a few months later, in April 2001, the CFCI claimed an instrumental role in bringing the provincial government, First Nations, environmental groups, forestry companies, and local communities to endorse a framework for the future of the Great Bear Rainforest. Formalized in the government's announcement of an Interim Economic Measures arrangement with local First Nations, and its release of an Interim Land Use Plan for the Central Coast, this agreement, described by the provincial premier as a "hard-won consensus aimed at saving areas of global significance" was met with widespread (if not universal) goodwill. In principle the agreement envisaged the establishment of protected areas, the implementation of ecosystem-based management, the development of a new regional economy, and a commitment to government-to-government relationships between BC and eight First Nations. Yet this was a framework, not a final document; parts of the deal were vague and much was left open to later negotiation.[20] Two and four years on, despite some reduction in the annual wood harvest and the protection of twenty large valleys, environmental leaders were dissatisfied at the continuation of business-as-usual logging practices and the slow implementation of ecologically sensitive forest management.

Meanwhile, after a great deal of biophysical and socio-economic research, gathering of traditional knowledge, the establishment of a Conservation Investments and Incentives Initiative to attract financing (that would both allow conservation and promote economic development), and thousands of hours of committee work, the way was paved for a final Great Bear Rainforest Agreement in February 2006.[21] This agreement had three important facets. First, some 21,120 square kilometres (one-third of the land area of the central and northern coasts), encompassing a wide range of habitat types and almost 40 percent of the mature forest, were protected under new conservancy legislation drafted to meet the needs of First Nations and environmental groups. Second, all parties agreed to the full implementation, beyond these areas and within three years, of Ecosystem-Based Management practices intended to meet the needs of conservation and community stability at a regional scale.[22] And third, a Coastal Opportunities Fund of $120 million was established, with half the total provided by philanthropic sources dedicated to conservation management, science, and stewardship jobs in First Nations communities, and the remainder, contributed equally by federal and provincial governments, designated for investment in sustainable business ventures in First Nations' territories and communities.

These were momentous achievements in the span of a single decade, and they reflected a new order of things. In place of activism aimed simply and directly at the protection of nature – by physically preventing machinery from cutting down trees in specific valleys – in the Great Bear Rainforest activists intervened in the complex commodity chains linking forests to producers, retailers, and consumers around the globe. In place of attempts to create wilderness parks that excluded productive activities, in the Great Bear Rainforest environmentalists worked to create new economies within the heart of a protected area. Where environmental groups once denounced loggers as enemies of nature, in the Great Bear Rainforest they worked with forestry companies to improve the way that they cut down trees. Where environmental campaigns once represented indigenous people as the continent's first ecologists or earth stewards, in the Great Bear Rainforest environmentalists recognized First Nations as governments with legitimate interests in the use and ownership of the earth and its resources.

As an outcome of these sea changes in environmental and social attitudes, the Great Bear Rainforest Agreement has drawn widespread attention. More may have been written about the Clayoquot protests than about the establishment of the Great Bear Rainforest, but the latter has drawn a far wider range of interest, as activists, resource managers, business consultants, the leaders of indigenous groups and ENGOS, and scholars trained in several disciplines have sought inspiration, guidance, wisdom, meaning – and perhaps even career advancement – in their examination of the mid-coast/Great Bear Rainforest debate. Some of this outpouring is opaque and a fair part of it, published in academic journals but perhaps best described as a form of "higher journalism" written amid the fray, is likely to be superseded. Still, the best and most thoughtful work on the "ongoing revolution" that is the Great Bear Rainforest – and this volume is part of that – has much to tell us. So, to take but one example, scholars interested in furthering social innovation, such as Ola Tjornbo, Frances Westley, and Darcy Riddell of the University of Waterloo, have seen unfolding events on the mid-coast/Great Bear Rainforest as breaking new ground in efforts to tackle "the highly complex and critical problems societies are increasingly coming to face around the globe."[23] This is no small thing. Moreover, they argue, an understanding of how those involved in transforming approaches to resource management on the mid-coast were able to bring this change about is vital to developing the "knowledge, and ultimately tools that may help many more such complex negotiations to occur in the future."

This is precisely where Justin Page makes his contribution in *Tracking the Great Bear*. Conjuring an innovative opening to his book, he plunges readers into the "dense tangle of ecological, economic, social, and political relations" out of which the Great Bear Rainforest was and is constituted in its many incarnations. Recognizing that much was in flux on the BC coast at the turn of the millennium, he is mindful of the observation, by French science and technology studies scholar Bruno Latour, that "in situations where innovations proliferate, where group boundaries are uncertain, [and] when the range of entities to be taken into account fluctuates," then conventional forms of explanation are inadequate to the task of understanding events. In response, his pioneering contribution avoids the assumptions and analytic techniques built up in the analysis of earlier conflicts. Rather than run through another social constructionist analysis of the meanings assigned to places, prepare another political economic account of the capture of policy by industry, or offer another description of the mobilization of resources within policy windows by environmentalists, in the manner of much social movements analysis, Page chooses simply to "follow the actors themselves" to learn "how environmentalists gained the power to influence land-use decisions in British Columbia" (pp. 7, 13, and 12 herein), thereby fashioning a new amalgam of nature and society on BC's coast.

Simply following the actors is no recipe for a simple history, however. Page proceeds deliberately, analytically, and from a particular standpoint. Trained in sociology, Page is well-schooled in current efforts within the environmental social sciences to move beyond the long-standing intellectual separation of society and nature to emphasize, instead, the hybridity of the human and non-human spheres (sometimes marked as socio-nature). He also draws intellectual inspiration from the work of Latour, Michel Callon, and John Law that regards "everything in the social and natural worlds as a continuously generated effect of the webs of relations within which they are located." Following this lead, Page systematically deploys the conceptual approach known as actor-network theory (ANT) to argue that the environmentalists' success in the Great Bear Rainforest rested on their ability to assemble a network of disparate elements that "act[ed] as a single unit of force" (pp. 11, 10 herein).

Much has been written about actor-network theory and many before Justin Page have adopted its insights in efforts to better understand particular circumstances. Yet both the status and the value of ANT are matters of continuing debate. One of its main proponents has described it as a "semiotic machine for waging war on essential differences" and another has said that ANT is "simply another way ... of being faithful to the insights of ethnomethodology."[24] It is perhaps better regarded as a "sensibility" than a "theory," as "an orientation to the world that brings certain characteristics into view."[25] Among these are an acceptance of the "constitutive role of non-humans in the fabric of social life" and the conviction that "agency is distributed," which is to say that actors and their networks are mutually constitutive and that things get done through assemblages of social and material entities rather than because subjects or objects act in isolation. Critics of this approach charge that it pays too little heed to questions of race, class, and gender, and that it underestimates the role of power in society. Some suggest that it is ultimately purely descriptive and that its main point seems to be that everything is connected. Others are skeptical because some deployments of ANT trace such complex patterns of causality that they seem to obfuscate rather than clarify the problem at hand.[26]

Webs or networks – "groups of actors connected by social ties or relationships" – are everywhere, of course, and it is important to emphasize that ANT conceives of networks as "more than social" entities.[27] From this perspective, networks include a markedly wide range of participants. Human and non-human elements are afforded equal consideration and potential to act within markedly "heterogeneous" networks. Reflecting this, the term "actant" is sometimes used instead of "actor" to describe network participants that might include men and microbes, ideas and tools, women and shellfish, chisels and sewage systems. ANT networks also encompass a great diversity of dynamic, reciprocal, and open-ended relationships. Rather than mapping the ties that bind individuals – charting the structure of pre-existing relationships – ANT practitioners seek to discover the ways in which actors "define and distribute roles, and mobilize or invent others to play these roles."[28]

Because actor-networks have many links and nodes, and because they are contingent, flexible, heterogeneous, and to some degree informal, they commonly overlap and take different forms depending upon the scale at or criteria by which they are defined.[29] Page is well aware of this and acknowledges that his account of the establishment of the Great Bear Rainforest focuses on the network-building efforts of environmentalists. This (environmentalists') network intersected with many others. But it was not conjoint with any of them. So Page's story of the Great Bear Rainforest is one among several. Had his point of entry into this maze of overlapping networks been other than the one he chose, his account of developments focused on the mid-coast would have been different from the one now before you.

At some level, of course, this is self-evident. Different accounts of the Great Bear stage afford more or less influential roles to those who played upon it.[30] Civil servants who toiled far from the media spotlight give some prominence to the CCLRMP process, the role of government in orchestrating it, and the readiness of the forest industry to adjust; First Nations note the importance of their willingness to participate in discussions; corporate leaders stress the importance of their vision and leadership; and some say little would have been accomplished without the work of expert facilitators and the staff of the Hollyhock Leadership Institute who counselled environmental group representatives about the value of mindfulness, meditation, and the need to move beyond confrontation. In the end, of course, this is a large part of Page's point – that what we take as reality is shaped by the networks that help to constitute it – and (he would insist as a corollary) that "a network approach digs deeply into the dynamics of power" (p. 124 herein).

Following Page as he tracks the multiple strands of the environmentalist network through the Great Bear Rainforest debates, one is reminded of Latour's assertion that "the idea of network is the Ariadne's thread of ... interwoven stories" tying them together in a way that is "more supple than the notion of system, more historical than the notion of structure, [and] more empirical than the notion of complexity."[31] Developed to provide insight into the development of science and technology, early work using the ANT approach focused on the complex interwoven stories that linked governments, boardrooms, laboratories, ideas, money, people, and technologies. Here Page deals with the interwoven stories of First Nations, forestry workers, corporate leaders, environmental activists, trees, bears, maps, government officials, local residents, distant consumers of BC forest products, landscapes, land-use and resource policies, and local deployments of ideas about risk, scale, and time, conservation, development, and justice. By examining these through an ANT lens, Justin Page provides a strong empirical account of an important episode in environmental conflict in BC, and provides a fresh, forward-looking perspective that deepens our understanding of contemporary environmentalism. There is much of value here, not only about the re-conceptualization of an extensive timber supply area as a giant wilderness park and then as a space where environmental preservation, forestry reform, and the recognition of indigenous rights could be implemented side by side, but also about how people act in the world and the relations between society and nature.

Tracking the Great Bear is a splendid title for this pithy book, because the idea of the Great Bear Rainforest was, and remains, absolutely central to what happened on this coast. As Tzeporah Berman (who was centrally involved in the early Great Bear Rainforest campaign) and a few others recognized near the beginning of the Clayoquot protests, building interest in the environmentalist cause required its leaders "to think like storytellers."[32] Above all else, they "needed to create a narrative to frame ... [their] work, to engage people, to capture interest and focus attention."[33] Stories can be powerful coagulants and compelling motivators. They articulate the ties that embed people in networks. They allow people to understand their place in the larger scheme of things and to appreciate how particular actions, however small they may seem, help to move the plot forward. But the plot is rarely constant. Events are contingent, and the stories signalled by the "Great Bear Rainforest" label have changed markedly in the two decades or so that it has been in circulation.

Against this backdrop, it is worth reflecting on the role that stories play in shaping environmental action. According to Raul Lejano, Mrill Ingram, and Helen Ingram, recent advocates for doing just this through an approach that they call narrative-network analysis, the stories that protesters tell about their involvement with environmental movements can reveal much about how networks are created and sustained. By studying stories and groupings of actors (or networks) simultaneously, they claim to better understand the "the quality of arrangements, complex motivations and relational knowledge that sustain attachment to environmental causes."[34] In this view, "narratives are part of the glue that binds networks" and attending to them enhances our understanding of how and why those involved in events created "new stories about their motivations, as well as the science, ethics and values informing their environmental practices."[35]

Page does not use the term narrative-network analysis and would eschew the social constructionist implications often associated with that phrase. Yet *Tracking the Great Bear* surely lays the groundwork for thinking productively along some of the lines sketched by Lejano, Ingram, and Ingram in their discussion of this approach. By documenting the transition from fiercely confrontational, oppositional activism to a more inclusive, collaborative, collective form of environmental politics in the development of the Great Bear Rainforest Agreement, this book shows how all of those involved in discussions, negotiations, and actions pertaining to the mid- and north coasts of BC worked out new ways of relating to (or framed new stories about) the rainforest environment and each other. By moving beyond familiar binary conceptualizations – such as those between nature and society, science and politics, ecology and economy, and local and global – this book also challenges widely accepted ways of thinking about (storying) the environment.

To put this another way: earlier environmentalist conceptions – of the forest industry as the serpent in BC's rainforest garden, and common "Paradise Lost narratives" that indicted humanity's destructive impacts on (pristine) environments – depended upon a particular, purified way of seeing that pitted the interests of ecology and economy against each other and drew a rigid distinction between exploitative humankind and vulnerable "nature" in need of protection.

The Great Bear Rainforest Agreement is undergirded by a very different set of assumptions. Because all involved in reaching the agreement made concessions, it has sometimes been described as a compromise. But this has unnecessarily negative connotations. Letting go of particular commitments opens the way to embrace others, and in Page's telling, the story of the Great Bear Rainforest invites us to do exactly that. At one level it is empowering because it suggests that the development of compelling, inclusive narratives and strategic interventions in networks may have greater potential to transform existing ways of thinking and acting than the once-common strategy of identifying foes and demonizing them. This way leads to important gains in what some have called ecological democracy. At a second level, Page's detailed demonstration of the importance of collaboration and co-existence for advancing the conservation economy enshrined in the 2006 agreement drives home the importance of rethinking the human-nature relationship to transcend the long-standing divide between "ephemeral human political interests" on the one hand and the "cold, hard non-human scientific facts" on the other (p. 90 herein). This way leads to a more just and environmentally sustainable future, a future foreshadowed by some of the developments discussed in this book and realizable, in its author's estimation, by the remaking of the very idea of conservation that they portend. May the tracks to the "one good common world" indeed lead through the Great Bear Rainforest of British Columbia, as Justin Page hopes and has explored so intriguingly.

Acknowledgments

A book, they say, is a collective endeavour; this book takes the aphorism literally. To tell the story of the Great Bear Rainforest – in a way that is coherent, defensible, interesting, and useful – I have gathered together a great number of materials from many sources. This story, like all stories, depends for its existence on countless contributors. First, I would like to acknowledge the bears, salmon, trees, human cultures, and other living and non-living beings located along British Columbia's central and north coasts. I would also like to recognize my interviewees: the environmental activists, First Nations, forestry representatives, and government officials who graciously gave of their time to pour over more than ten years of conflict, negotiation, science, and politics, all of which greatly aided my understanding of the making of the Great Bear Rainforest. I would especially like to thank Ian McAllister who allowed me to quote from our interviews as well as from *The Great Bear Rainforest: Canada's Forgotten Coast*, a book he co-authored with Karen McAllister. I am indebted to the trail of electronic and paper sources about the Great Bear Rainforest that have allowed me to piece together the complex scientific, cultural, political, and economic networks comprising it. Commentators on and intellectual supporters of early drafts, including Thomas Kemple, Ralph Matthews, Terre Satterfield, and Steven Petrina, were instrumental. Later commentators, who shaped the book in a variety of ways, included Stewart Lockie, Trevor Barnes, and Jeremy Rayner. I would also like to thank the two anonymous reviewers of the manuscript whose insightful comments I have done my best to incorporate. UBC Press has been supportive throughout, and I particularly appreciate the editorial contributions of Graeme Wynne and the guidance of Randy Schmidt. Finally, I would like to reserve special thanks for my key reader, soul supporter, and life partner: thank you, Maryam Nabavi.

Abbreviations

ANT	actor-network theory
CAD	conservation area design
CCLRMP	Central Coast Land Resource Management Plan
CFCI	Coast Forest Conservation Initiative
CIII	Conservation Investments and Incentives Initiative
CIT	Coast Information Team
COFI	Council of Forest Industries
EBM	ecosystem-based management
ENGO	environmental non-governmental organization
GBR	Great Bear Rainforest
Interfor	International Forest Products
IWA	Industrial Wood and Allied Workers of Canada
JSP	Joint Solutions Project
Kit-Git-Pit	Kitasoo-Gitga'at Protocol Implementation Team
LRMP	Land and Resource Management Plan
LUP	land-use plan
OPP	obligatory point of passage
PIMCs	Plan Implementation Committees
RSP	Rainforest Solutions Project
WCWC	Western Canada Wilderness Committee

Tracking the Great Bear

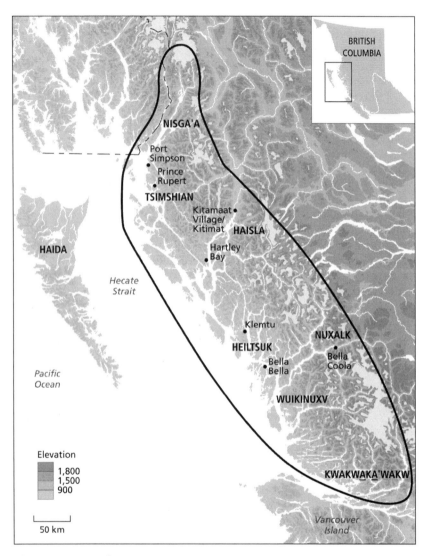

The Great Bear Rainforest

Introduction

It is February 7, 2006. You sit down in front of the television, or spread out a newspaper, or maybe listen to the radio in your car. You might be in Vancouver, Montreal, or New York. Or you might be in England or Austria, perhaps Japan. You learn that an agreement has been reached to protect the world's "largest remaining temperate coastal rainforest." There's a good chance that you haven't heard of this place. You're told that environmentalists call it the Great Bear Rainforest and that it is in Canada, where it stretches along British Columbia's central and north coasts. To help you understand the vastness of this new protected area, the Great Bear Rainforest's size is compared to more familiar land masses, depending on where you live. It may be described as almost the size of New Jersey, twice the size of Yellowstone, or three times the size of Prince Edward Island. The entire area is twice the size of Belgium, they say. The agreement protects the habitat of species such as grizzly bears, wolves, salmon, and the "elusive spirit bear," says one reporter. It is "British Columbia's gift to the planet," says an environmentalist. "Spirit bear," you think, "that sounds pretty interesting."

※

Ending a decade-long environmental battle once dubbed the "War of the Woods," British Columbia is set to announce Tuesday the creation of a park twice the size of Yellowstone along a vast coastal swath where grizzly bears and wolves now prowl under thousand-year-old cedar trees.

– DOUGLAS STRUCK, *WASHINGTON POST* (2006)

An improbable assemblage of officials from the provincial government,
coastal Native Canadian nations, logging companies and environmental
groups will announce an agreement to preserve the home of the Spirit
bear, which is also the largest remaining temperate coastal rain forest.

– CLIFFORD KRAUSS, *NEW YORK TIMES* (2006A)

❧

Reading on, you learn that this "unprecedented collaboration between
First Nations, industry, environmentalists, local governments, and many
other stakeholders" (British Columbia 2006) produced an agreement to
protect 1.8 million hectares of coastal rainforest while putting in place
strict, lighter-touch forestry practices for 4.6 million hectares, bringing
the total area encompassed by the agreement to 6.4 million hectares. The
reporter notes that the hundred protected valleys specified in the agreement represent about one-third of the area, while about two-thirds remain
open to logging. "I thought this story was about an agreement to protect
wilderness," you might think, "but now they're talking about how most
of the place will be logged!"

You need to visualize the place referred to, so you do a web search for
a map. You come up with two different versions of the same place. The
first map, on the Sierra Club's website, corresponds to your initial reaction
to the story. Environmental groups have drawn a big circle around a swath
of remote, rugged land. The map shows no signs of human use or habita-
tion. The second map, released by the BC government along with its
announcement of the land-use agreement, is more differentiated. It shows
protected areas but also empty spaces outside these protected areas. These
"operating areas," as they are referred to on the map, vastly outnumber
the protected areas. You go back to the news story. They are talking about
how the operating areas will be subject to a novel management regime
called ecosystem-based management (EBM). EBM, they say, is a way of
managing land that minimizes impact on the environment, thereby ensuring that resource use remains sustainable. Someone says that EBM guides
forestry planning on the basis of what you should leave, not what you
should take. That is, it shifts the focus from logging-centred parameters
such as fibre volume to ecosystem characteristics such as bear dens, tree
snags, and buffers around streams.

⁊₭

The new parks, in addition to 600,000 hectares already in parkland,
will create a network of protected areas encompassing 1.8 million
hectares – an area three times the size of Prince Edward Island –
in 100 pristine river valleys.

— GORDON HAMILTON, *VANCOUVER SUN* (2006)

Logging will be allowed in many areas in the Great Bear Rainforest, but
it will take place under "ecosystem-based management." The new logging
approach is supposed to protect the environment while permitting up to
50 per cent of the timber to be removed from some areas.

— MARK HUME, *GLOBE AND MAIL* (2006)

[Ecosystem-based management] integrates ecological, economic and
social purposes and is designed to work as a management and planning
regime that first looks at what is needed to be left in place to allow for a
healthy ecosystem and then looks at what can be taken out.

— RAINFOREST SOLUTIONS PROJECT (N.D.)

⁊₭

You might be getting the sense that this story is about forestry practices
as much as it is about nature conservation, and you might find this interesting because logging and the protection of nature are opposed in your
mind. But EBM seems to say that both things can be true: nature can be
preserved, and foresters can make money. Along these lines, you hear
something about the development of a new *conservation economy.* Environmentalists raised $60 million, matched by the provincial and (probably)
federal governments to total $120 million, to support the development of
a regional economy that creates employment while protecting wilderness.

Now you might be getting the sense that this story is about people as
much as it is about wilderness. Indeed, you hear that EBM has a "social"
aspect. This reminds you of a third map that you saw on the David Suzuki
Foundation website, entitled "Turning Point: First Nations Signatories to
the Protocol with British Columbia, April 4, 2001." You go back to take
a better look at it. This map, like the other ones, uses circles to claim areas

of land. But the circles do not encompass nature (as in the Great Bear Rainforest map) or human uses of nature (as in the land-use zoning map). Rather, they assert ownership, territory, home. Displaying the traditional territories of Haisla First Nation, Heiltsuk First Nation, and Tsimshian First Nation, the third map is the first to indicate human occupation.

First Nations assert strong claims on the land encompassed by the agreement. Like environmentalists, they are concerned with protecting the land from status quo industrial logging. But they are equally interested in developing new economic opportunities for their impoverished communities. The media report that First Nations endorse EBM and are keen on the idea of a conservation economy. Art Sterritt, the leader of a group called Coastal First Nations, talks about a diversified economy, First Nations' access to forestry, and the development of new economic opportunities such as ecotourism, fishing lodges, and shellfish. He says that, "for First Nations, [the agreement] is a new beginning. It means that we're going to be able to develop an economy that's sustainable, and that's really what's important about this" (as cited in Forsythe 2006).

"How in the world," you might be wondering, "did environmentalists (who usually focus on ecological preservation), logging companies (who generally concentrate on economic development), and First Nations (who often contest rights, title, and governance) ever agree on a common land-use plan?" There might be good reasons why the newspapers use descriptors such as "historic," "unprecedented," and "landmark" to describe the agreement. The war in the woods is over, say the newspapers, TVs, and radios. "This agreement brings an end to the long-standing resource-use conflicts over this land," says Dallas Smith, a First Nations leader (cited in British Columbia 2006). "This is a revolution in the way that we approach forestry in British Columbia," says Merran Smith (2006), an environmental representative. "It is a revolution where communities are leaders in their own destinies. Where logging practices have a lighter touch on the land and conservation comes first."

Remaking British Columbia's Coastal Forests

This book is about the (re)making of the Great Bear Rainforest (GBR). To open this exploration, I have deliberately thrown you into the *medias res* – the middle of things – with no guidance, framework, or sense of direction. There is no other way: this is always where we find ourselves, in one imbroglio or another. Within just a few introductory pages, something as simple as a new protected area has become a complete mystery, with multiple actors, themes, tensions, and questions. Seemingly about a "saved" wilderness – complete with towering trees, wolves, and bears – it is also about land rights, land-use practices, and the development of local economies. When one enters the Great Bear Rainforest, one encounters not a pristine wilderness but a dense tangle of ecological, economic, social, and political relations. *Tracking the Great Bear* traces the constitution and reconstitution of those relations to provide insight into the establishment of one of Canada's newest and most important protected areas.

When you are in the middle of things, you don't stay in one place for long. Things are always evolving, moving, and transforming. Just as you think you have a grip on the actors, interests, and themes, they shift their alliances and change their definitions. Accordingly, the only way to get a sense of the story is to jump in and follow the flow. If you already have ideas about who environmentalists are and what they want, what "wilderness" is, how Aboriginal rights are best achieved, or the goals of the forestry industry, please park these ideas here, or at least be prepared to have them challenged. As you become more deeply connected to this unique episode in Canadian environmental history, you might find that your own ways of understanding society and the environment have begun to shift and change.

※

It took a while for people to hash it out from "okay, we want no logging"
– which everybody might want in their hearts –
but there was enough people to say "well, we're not going to
achieve that, and is that really what we want?"

— INTERVIEW WITH AN ENVIRONMENTALIST

It took me a long time to realize that our conceptions of wilderness,
you know the basic conception of wilderness,
that it's a place untouched by humans, is really wrong.

— TZEPORAH BERMAN (INTERVIEWED ON *THE NATIONAL*,
CBC, JUNE 16, 1999)

The reality is we've been out and visited those First Nations
communities, and they're ... in trouble, like, it's not good out there.
These people – something has to shift.

— INTERVIEW WITH AN ENVIRONMENTALIST

It felt like what we're coming up with was a big vision.
You know, we're going to protect the majority of all the intact valleys,
and we're going to transform the logging practices, and we're going
to create a new kind of economy.

– INTERVIEW WITH AN ENVIRONMENTALIST

ૠ

I have referred to the GBR as a "story." I do not mean to suggest that the place called the GBR is fictional or that its primary actors are mere characters. I use the term to highlight the multiple forms that the GBR takes through its mobilization in media clips, maps, and the words of its key actors. The GBR is a real place, one that also flows as words, images, data, wood, and people (all of which are also real and traceable) among a global network of actors. Each instantiation of the multiple GBR is a variation with its own specific reality, and each can be traced back to its material-semiotic source(s) in and around British Columbia's central and north coasts. This book too is a variation of the GBR – a story written in the genre of environmental sociology.

Environmental sociologists study the social causes and consequences of environmental issues and problems as well as social responses to those problems (e.g., Redclift and Woodgate 2010). In the area of natural resource management, environmental sociologists tend to focus on how natural resources are defined and represented, the structural causes of resource depletion, the unequal impacts of resource management decisions on marginalized groups, and the strategies, tactics, and networks of the environmental movement. In these terms, the GBR is a ripe case for sociological study. As an example of collaborative natural resource management, the GBR yields insights into the devolution of decision-making power from experts to stakeholders, contests over representations of natural systems, the distribution of costs and benefits of conservation, and the role of markets and coalitions in the environmental movement. Much value is derived from this form of study (e.g., Clapp 2004; Cullen et al. 2010; Davis 2009; Frame, Gunton, and Day 2004; Hayter 2003; Howlett, Rayner, and Tollefson 2009; Jackson and Curry 2004; Low and Shaw 2011; McGee, Cullen, and Gunton 2010; Rayner and Zittoun 2008; Rossiter 2004; Shaw 2004).

However, environmental sociology's self-definition as the critical study of "societal-environmental interactions" (Catton and Dunlap 1978) subtly impedes appreciation of the GBR's most interesting feature: its dissolution of a presumed boundary "between" nature and society. Despite the rich and diverse range of epistemological views espoused in the field (from realist to social constructivist to critical realist), environmental sociology continues to rest on an underlying assumption that society and environment are separate if "interacting" domains. Not surprisingly, this focus confines researchers to the social and political dimensions of environmental issues and problems – sociologists' area of expertise – while leaving non-human processes to natural scientists. This methodological restriction manifests itself in sociological debates over the compatibility of conservation and development. Regardless of whether sociologists argue for a basic incompatibility of conservation and development under conditions of advanced capitalism, or for the possibility of reconciliation under processes of ecological modernization, analyses tend to focus on the operation of social institutions without considering the role of non-humans therein.

Recent years have seen increasing attempts within the environmental social sciences to avoid dichotomies between society and nature, conservation and development, and science and politics to account instead for the emergence of new *social natures* or novel, hybrid configurations of humans and non-humans (Braun and Castree 1998; Castree and Braun 2001; White and Wilbert 2009). *Tracking the Great Bear* seeks to bring these scholarly developments more fully within environmental sociology by unpacking the GBR as a powerful hybrid assemblage of humans and non-humans. This project builds on existing scholarship on British Columbia's entrenched top-down, timber-biased policy "compact" between government and industry and the struggles by social actors such as environmentalists and First Nations to create policy changes (Cashore 2001; Hayter 2003; Marchak 1983; Markey et al. 2005; Wilson 1998). However, this book provides a novel analysis of British Columbia's war in the woods. Like other sociologically informed accounts, it focuses on power struggles among social groups as they vie to influence land-use policies. However, rather than analyzing such struggles in traditionally sociological terms (using concepts such as social movement mobilization, political opportunity windows, discursive practices, or economic and ideological power), I focus on environmentalists' strategies to reassemble the scientific, cultural, political, and economic networks constituting British Columbia's coastal forests.

ASSEMBLING ACTOR-NETWORKS TO SAVE THE WILDERNESS

> *Think of Roscoe Inlet [an inlet in the Great Bear Rainforest]
> as the hub of a wheel, with spokes that reach all the way to
> the premier's office, the corporate headquarters of logging
> multinationals, the foreign offices of some of B.C. wood
> exporters' largest customers, the influential command centres
> of the most affluent philanthropic foundations in the U.S.,
> environmental groups and First Nation chiefs and their
> councils. It has brought long-standing combatants to the
> table to discuss, on more or less equal terms, the future of
> what is now widely recognized as one of the last great
> terrestrial conservation opportunities on the globe.*
>
> – *Andrew Findlay*, BC Business Online *(2007)*

The principal aim of this book is to explain how environmentalists established the Great Bear Rainforest in an area that is materially and politically aligned with the interests of the forestry industry. The book's central proposition is that environmentalists achieved success by assembling a powerful actor-network, an assemblage of disparate elements that act as a single unit of force (Callon 1986). Scholarship that makes use of this concept, loosely grouped under the label of actor-network theory (ANT), was originally established to explain the development of scientific knowledge and technology. Working within the small field of science and technology studies, Bruno Latour, Michel Callon, and John Law (Callon 1980, 1986; Callon and Latour 1981; Callon and Law 1982; Latour 1987, 1988; Law 1986) disputed the "discovery" account of science and technology, the view that great scientists and engineers combine institutionalized methods and individual genius to uncover the truths of nature and to develop superior technologies. They also went a step further than the alternative view that science and technology are ultimately reducible to social and political factors. Taking a more expansive view, they suggested that scientists and engineers routinely crisscross multiple scientific, economic, political, and cultural domains. If we want to understand how scientific knowledge or

technologies are produced, they argued, then we need to examine protag-
onists' network-building activities everywhere that they occur.

More than a novel epistemological view of how experts come to know
nature and the workings of machines, ANT espouses the ontological
position that reality itself is the outcome of networks. Inspired by Julien
Greimas's theory of semiotics, Michel Serres's philosophy of translation,
and the process philosophies of Alfred North Whitehead and Gilles
Deleuze, the actor-network concept rests on a relational ontology that
"treat[s] everything in the social and natural worlds as a continuously
generated effect of the webs of relations within which they are located"
(Law 2008, 142). The "object" of scientific knowledge is not "out there,"
complete in itself and waiting to be discovered; rather, it is enrolled as a
network-building participant. Only after the socio-natural network has
been assembled can one point to a definite reality with particular features
and attributes. This is not to say that nothing pre-exists human-orchestrated
network-building activities (indeed, there needs to be something to enrol
in the network). Rather, it means that the usual distinctions between reality
and representation, nature and society, science and politics, the material
and the symbolic, and even epistemology and ontology do not apply. In
their place is the process of heterogeneous network construction.

While not without its critics (e.g., Amsterdamska 1990; Bloor 1999a,
1999b; Fuller 2007; Winner 1993), ANT's conceptual tools are increasingly
being recognized for their applicability to the analysis of environmental
issues (e.g., Besel 2011; Bled 2010; Blok 2010a, 2010b; Dempsey 2011; Eden
2009; Holifield 2009; Jepson, Buckingham, and Barua 2011; Jolivet and
Heiskanen 2010; Landström et al. 2011; Lien and Law 2011; Lockie 2007;
Rodger, Moore, and Newsome 2009; Rodríguez-Giralt 2011; Sodero 2011;
Thoms 2011; Whatmore 2009). Most environmental issues, including forest
protection, involve highly complex mixtures of scientific knowledge, political
struggles, economic interests, social concerns, and non-human constituents.
Often environmental battles are fought as if the issues can be separated into
one true biophysical reality, on one side, and social groups with competing
interests, values, and knowledge, on the other. However, it takes little prob-
ing of most environmental controversies to discover that our understanding
of biophysical reality turns out to be just as contested as its value and use.
Adding more science to the mix usually does little to resolve the issue and
often makes it even more contested. Indeed, the separation of complex
issues into nature versus society is a general tactic and resource used by
participants in environmental struggles – and not a feature of the terrain
itself. ANT allows researchers to dive into the complexity of environmental

issues while treating concepts such as nature and society as topics in need of explanation rather than as explanatory resources themselves.

Tracking the Great Bear deploys conceptual tools offered by ANT to achieve three objectives. First, by refusing to limit the analysis to social and political dimensions while treating biophysical categories such as the rainforest as given, the book provides a unique, comprehensive, and detailed account of how environmentalists gained the power to influence land-use decisions in British Columbia. Second, by strictly following the methodological practice of tracing network-building activities wherever they occur, rather than using the speedier but potentially inaccurate approach of relying on pre-existing concepts and frameworks of explanation, the book demonstrates the fresh and novel ways in which relationships between humans and non-humans were worked out in this particular case. Third, by providing a full-scale ANT analysis of a sociologically important environmental issue, the book demonstrates the value of ANT to environmental sociology.

Reassembling Methods

⁊

Imagine that I am a traveller and that I just arrived here after travelling around the world. I've heard about this place called the "Great Bear Rainforest," and I'm intrigued, but I don't really know anything about it. I was told that I should talk to you because you do know a lot about it. So, here I am! Can you describe the "Great Bear Rainforest" to me?

- What's special or significant about the place?
- What would you say are its most distinctive features?
- What's your own connection with the place?

— SELECTION FROM AUTHOR'S INTERVIEW QUESTIONS

⁊

Before proceeding to the analysis, I ought to re-emphasize that this book reassembles a particular version of the GBR. This account, like all social science research, is subject to the usual standards of objectivity, validity, and generalizability; these methodological principles, however, are slightly recast in ANT terms. My account is objective in the sense that it is full of objects or materials traceable back to the people, places, and things associated with the GBR (I have already introduced some of these elements in the quotations interspersed in this introduction). The material that I draw on includes agreements (land and resource management plans, government-First Nations, ENGOs-industry, etc.), terms of reference, work plans, legal orders, presentations, reports (technical, organizational, workshop), scientific articles, ecological data, newsletters, press releases, news stories, public and customer information materials, campaign materials, histories and timelines, minutes and agendas of meetings, maps, videos, films, and radio interviews. I also conducted thirty-four in-depth semi-structured interviews with key actors between September and December, 2007, whom I purposefully selected from environmental organizations, forestry companies, First Nations organizations, and local and provincial government departments.[1]

The evidence on which I base my claims also provides a basis for actors to object to what is said about them (and for me to defend my claims). The validity of my analysis is ultimately dependent on how it stands up in the hands of those most intimately associated with the case. On that score, interviewees provided with earlier versions of this book have not objected to anything said about them or the case. However, it is important to note that the analysis is not objective in the sense of providing an impartial, synoptic, god's-eye view of the one true GBR. Nor was that my goal. My goal was to "follow the actors themselves" (Latour 2005b) to learn how the GBR was established. The analysis is *symmetrical* in the sense that I consider both the "social" and the "natural," and the "political" and the "scientific," with the same analytical repertoire (Callon 1986). However, in another sense, the analysis is *asymmetrical.*

Science and technology studies scholars have criticized ANT for failing to recognize that researchers inevitably privilege some actors and elements over others, arguing that (1) it is impossible to account simultaneously for all network elements (particularly those of which we remain unaware) and (2) researchers connect materially and symbolically to the networks that they study in necessarily partial ways (Lee and Brown 1994; Star 1991). My account is asymmetrical because I have self-consciously chosen to explore the establishment of the GBR from the perspectives of environmentalists. This does not mean that I restrict my analysis to their interpretations of the case but that I examine their network-building activities (whether they are explicitly aware of network building or not). This involves going well beyond environmentalists' interpretations to take account of the wide range of human and non-human elements brought together by their interventions. Nevertheless, had the analysis proceeded from the perspectives of other network elements – whether First Nations, forestry workers, or grizzly bears – a somewhat different network would emerge and a different story be told.

I chose to follow environmentalists' interventions for practical reasons (I had to choose *some* point of entry into the network), for social scientific reasons (environmentalists influenced BC environmental policy in important ways that need to be *explained*), and for political reasons (I largely *agree* with environmentalists' goals to protect the ecological integrity of coastal British Columbia and other places around the world). With respect to the last point, this book represents a material and symbolic intervention in environmentalists' GBR network. Materially, it functions as a device with which to extend the GBR network to other people and places, where it might be translated and utilized in struggles over conservation. Symbolically, the book frames and characterizes the GBR network according to my academic interests, particularly my desire to influence the environmental community to reorient their thinking away from a "nature" versus "society" framework and toward a framework focused on the careful re-fashioning of collectives of humans and non-humans. The generalizability of my analysis will depend on the extent to which it is taken up and circulated to other places and contexts as well as the degree of its immutability in the hands of its recipients.

Outline of the Book

I have arranged the material in a rough chronological order beginning in the early 1990s, when environmentalists first became interested in British Columbia's central and north coasts, and ending with the agreement of 2006. Chapter 1 examines environmentalists' scientific and political re-definition of the coastal forests in terms amenable to their policy ambition, which, at the time, was the designation of British Columbia's central and north coasts as a giant park. I detail environmentalists' work to displace the official definition of the coastal forests by placing the forests in a wider ecological and cultural context. The official definition – the "Mid-Coast Timber Supply Area" – derives from a long-standing policy compact between industry and government and highlights an instrumental view of the forests. I show how environmentalists contested this view by creating a chain of associations that (1) designated a new, globally rare forest type termed the "coastal temperate rainforest," (2) used this designation to identify key threatened watersheds at the local resource management scale, (3) populated these watersheds with culturally resonant stories and images, and (4) rebranded the coastal forests as the Great Bear Rainforest, a name materially and symbolically loaded with scientific and political content.

Chapter 2 traces environmentalists' efforts to assemble a network in support of the redefined forests and the concomitant power shift between environmentalists and the BC forestry industry. I focus on a series of interventions aimed at translating the interests and identities of multiple actors. First, I describe how members of the BC environmental movement were enticed to refocus their efforts from isolated valleys in the southern portion of the province to the large area to the north. Second, I examine how grizzly bears were made to speak on behalf of the rainforests (instead of government and industry) through environmentalists' biology-based conservation plan. Third, I detail environmentalists' campaign against companies such as Home Depot, Staples, and IKEA (retail customers of BC forestry products), examining how these businesses were induced to demand reform in BC forestry practices as a condition of doing business with BC forestry companies.

Chapter 3 examines the shifting centre of gravity from government to environmentalists for land-use policy making. My central focus is on the uptake of, and resistance to, environmentalists' vision for the coastal forests and the consequent translation of that vision by a number of policy actors. First, I show how forestry companies worked to recapture their policy influence by recasting themselves as a conservation-oriented coalition. Second, I examine the translation of environmentalists' identities and interests as they negotiated with industry in a hybrid industry-environmentalist policy-making coalition. Third, I detail local communities' and First Nations' resistance to this unofficial policy process. Through an examination of multiple negotiations involved, I document the translation of environmentalists' original goal of creating a giant park into a plan to achieve conservation, *plus* forestry reform, *plus* Aboriginal rights and title (including the Aboriginal right to economic development).

Chapter 4 presents the principles and procedures invented by the actors to reconcile conservation, development, and justice in the evolving plan. Examining a pilot First Nations EBM project, I highlight three sets of mediating mechanisms designed to avoid trade-offs among these domains. The first set of mechanisms is conceptual: I trace environmentalists' deployment of the concepts of risk, scale, and time within an EBM framework to reconcile ecological protection with resource extraction. The second set is economic: I trace environmentalists' efforts to raise $120 million in funds to support a new "conservation economy" that translates conservation into economic development and economic development into conservation. The third set is political: I examine the development of protocols and agreements that institutionalize a new "government-to-government" relationship between First Nations and the government of British Columbia, thereby articulating justice with conservation and development.

The conclusion considers the implications of *Tracking the Great Bear* for natural resource management and environmental sociology. First, I discuss how environmentalists developed the power to devise an alternative procedure to official land-use planning via their problematization of the coastal forests, enrolment of actors, and innovations to articulate the interests of various actors. In this discussion, I highlight (1) power generation through network formation, (2) blending of science and politics and the material and symbolic, (3) non-human agency, and (4) the relationship "between" nature and society. Second, I argue that ANT provides a useful methodological reorientation for environmental sociology, providing it with a strong alternative to approaches resulting in realism/social constructivism debates. Rather than confining analysis to social structures, forces, and processes – which are subsequently related to nature (real or socially constructed) – I suggest that ANT discloses the structures and forces produced by the actors themselves to order human and non-human elements. Moreover, I suggest, ANT researchers participate in the networks that they study by rendering networks explicit and interpreting their ordering. Rather than theorizing the relationship between nature and society, ANT scholars follow the ways in which this issue is settled by the actors whom they study, while advocating for the democratic inclusion of all relevant actors.

By the end of the book, readers will have learned much about how the GBR project was originally conceived and how it evolved. Having jumped into the *medias res,* readers will have travelled great distances: with environmentalists as they pulled together concepts and data from British Columbia's coasts and elsewhere, (re)defining the GBR as a new type of forest; with bears as they protested outside forestry companies' offices and travelled around North America and Europe; with activists as they traced and intervened in the commodity chain linking forests, forestry companies, and retail customers; with forestry companies as they joined environmentalists in a joint project; with First Nations as they translated the emerging network into their own terms; and with stakeholders and experts as they worked to redefine ecology and economy. By the end of the account, readers will have witnessed the emergence of a new socio-material network and will have had the opportunity to examine in detail the work that it performed to generate power, intertwine science and politics, and redefine the relationship between society and nature.

I

Where in the World
Is the Great Bear?

Problematizing British Columbia's Coastal Forests

When I began my research for this book, the first thing that I discovered was the relational nature of time and place. As I unearthed historical materials and sifted through actors' recollections, I was transported to British Columbia's mid-coast in 1990s. To my surprise, once "there" I found that the place that I was looking for did not exist. Although this was the area that would become the Great Bear Rainforest, there were no maps, no books, no news releases, no websites to indicate this. There wasn't even an agreement – or a failure to reach an agreement. As far as environmentalists went, no one seemed to be around – nobody, that is, except for Wayne McCrory.

Since the mid-1980s, McCrory had been trying to encounter – and then protect – a white black bear. In an email communication of August 29, 2007, he told me that,

> along with Dr. Stephen Herrero and Ralph Archibald (a provincial bear biologist), we flew into a valley called the Khutzeymateen in a late fall storm in October in about 1985 after I/Valhalla Society received an anonymous envelope about a famous bear valley about to fall to the chain-saw and therein the story begins.

This story, like all stories, is multiple and mostly untold, so I can only scratch at a part of it. One of McCrory's stories has to do with his efforts to create Canada's first and only grizzly bear sanctuary as well as coastal British Columbia's first protected estuary (Khutzeymateen Grizzly Bear

Sanctuary was created in 1994 on British Columbia's north coast). But this is just the lead-in to another of his stories, one in which McCrory and some of his fellow "ursaphiles'" encountered, in Kitasoo and Gitga'at territories further to the south, a white bear. A press release in which McCrory's environmental group, the Valhalla Wilderness Society (2006), applauded the announcement of the 2006 agreement stated that

> eighteen years ago McCrory and a few of his colleagues were awe-struck by their first sighting of a white bear on Princess Royal Island. "We saw bears and salmon in every big and little valley, cathedral groves of giant Sitka spruce, and wolves on the beaches," says McCrory. "It was UNLOGGED and about as close to a wild bear heaven you could ever find on this earth."

Even earlier than McCrory, another non-Native person took up an interest in the mid-coast's white bears. In 1905, W.T. Hornady, a naturalist from the New York Zoological Society, described a white bear that had been spotted in a range spanning from River's Inlet in the south, to the Nass Valley in the north, and up the Skeena River to Hazelton in the east, but principally it concentrated on the islands and adjacent mainland on the north central coast. Hornady named the bear after Francis Kermode, an assistant to the director of the BC Museum of Natural History, calling it *Ursus americanus kermodei,* or Kermode American black bear. Hornady considered the bear to be a distinct species, but in 1928 it was reclassified as a sub-species of the black bear that contains a unique double recessive gene endowing what would otherwise be black bears with white fur. In the mid-1980s, McCrory and his colleagues searched for white Kermodes. After the "awe-inspiring" encounter in 1987, they developed a proposal for a conservancy, calling for the protection of 262,000 hectares on Princess Royal Island, smaller islands, and several valleys on adjacent mainland areas. They termed the proposed protected area the "Spirit Bear Conservancy," coming up with a name and an image that would have a large impact on the future development of the GBR. According to McCrory (2003), "the spirit bear became the international poster icon of the whole Great Bear Rainforest Campaign."

In the early 1990s, however, environmentalists had yet to frame British Columbia's coastal forests in these terms. The area was usually referred to as simply the "mid-coast." Sounding neutral enough, this name was actually associated with a long-standing policy compact between the provincial government and the forestry industry (Marchak 1983; Wilson 1998). The BC Ministry of Forests (2002) referred to the area as the Mid-Coast Timber

Supply Area, "an area of Crown land designated by the minister of forests in accordance with the Forest Act and managed for a range of objectives including timber production." In other words, what would one day become the Great Bear Rainforest was at this time understood primarily as a geographic location – the "mid-coast" – an area that contained a store of timber for the forestry industry, with possibly some other "objectives" tacked on.

Even in 1990s, this was not an uncontroversial definition. Beginning in the late 1960s and early 1970s, environmentalists and First Nations began to challenge the authority of the Crown to manage BC forests. Environmentalists argued that values other than timber production ought to be taken into account in forestry management, that voices other than industry ought to be part of the process, and that specific areas ought to be considered for protection (Wilson 1998). First Nations argued that their Aboriginal rights and title to historically unceded territories were being infringed by logging operations and government decisions. Government policy innovation in the 1970s, such as stakeholder involvement and multiple use policies, did little to quell a burgeoning war in the woods, however, since environmentalists considered these efforts inadequate and First Nations thought that their concerns were entirely sidelined. High-profile blockades of logging operations ensued in places such as Meares Island, South Moresby Island, the Stein Valley, and Clayoquot Sound. However, these protests took place almost exclusively in the southern portion of the province, far away from what was to become the Great Bear Rainforest.

So, as I began to dig into my historical research materials, all that I found for the place that was to become the Great Bear Rainforest were references to the Ministry of Forests and its "Mid-Coast Timber Supply Area," to McCrory and his "Spirit Bear Conservancy" proposal, and to First Nations and their "traditional territories." Otherwise, it was pretty quiet, except for some outdoor enthusiasts having fun paddling around in a couple of recreation areas (Fiordland Recreation Area and Hakai Protected Area had been established by Premier Bennett's Wilderness Advisory Committee in the mid-1980s). Although, around this time, things did heat up a bit in one area of the mid-coast – the Kitlope Valley. In the early 1990s, Ecotrust came all the way up from Portland to help the Heiltsuk oppose West Fraser Timber Company's plans to log the Kitlope Valley. Some of British Columbia's wilderness preservation groups became involved in that one, including the Sierra Club of Western Canada (now Sierra Club of BC), the Western Canada Wilderness Committee, and the Valhalla Wilderness Society (McCrory's group). They even managed to get the area designated as a conservancy, to be co-managed by the province and the Heiltsuk, in 1994.

Beyond these areas, there was really only one other small conflict in the region – the Koeye River Valley, adjacent to the Hakai Pass, in 1990. However, this one got Ian and Karen McAllister interested (another important story). MacMillan Bloedel was planning to log the valley, and a developer was planning to build a resort at the mouth of the river. Ian's father, Peter McAllister (a former director of the Sierra Club of Western Canada), organized a sailing trip to the Koeye River, inviting bear biologists, photographers, journalists, environmentalists, and his son. According to Ian and Karen McAllister (1997, 13),

> on the return journey through Queen Charlotte Sound, everyone on board fell silent as the obvious question moved through us like electricity. If the Koeye River could be so spectacular and yet so unrecognized, what about the eighty or ninety other river valleys on the mainland coast that were still intact and unprotected?

This is a pretty good framing device to get us thinking about the coast as a whole. And that's what the McAllisters started doing. Their coffee table book about the Great Bear Rainforest lets us see, through photographs, maps, and a narrative of their journey up and down the BC coast, "Canada's forgotten coast." Before they wrote it, British Columbia's central and north coasts were not singular. Rather, there were multiple, discrete elements – some environmental groups, the spirit bear, several forestry companies, a number of imperilled river valleys, and First Nations' traditional territories. In the absence of sustained attention from the wider environmental community, important elements comprising the coast were effectively "forgotten," and the default definition reigned. It would take several years and a great deal of scientific, economic, cultural, and political work before these coastal elements were (re)assembled into the object of an environmental campaign.

Constructing the Object of Environmental Politics

In 1996, when we started on this work, this area was known as the Mid-Coast Timber Supply Area, and the only value of this rainforest was dollars per cubic meter. Today, the Great Bear Rainforest is valued as an ecological legacy.

– Merran Smith, 2006

What is the "object" of environmental politics? Is it a material reality "out there" that needs to be brought "in here" and placed on the political agenda? Is it a set of beliefs that remains forever "in here" with no essential relation to reality "out there"? The view pursued in this book is that the object of environmental politics is a "thing" in the etymological sense of "a gathering or assemblage" (Latour 2005a). That is, the "thing" that comes to form the centre of environmental politics is produced when material, discursive, and collective elements are gathered in a format that gives this gathering some form of representation. In order for environmental groups to shift the understanding of British Columbia's coastal forests away from the Mid-Coast Timber Supply Area to something more amenable to their policy ambitions, they had to redefine or *problematize* (Callon 1986) the central and north coasts. In other words, they needed to draw together multiple and heterogeneous elements into a single, identifiable, and evocative "thing."

Neither the "object" of environmental politics nor its "subject" can be taken for granted. As noted above, there was no pre-existing group of environmentalists with interests in the central and north coasts. This group and their interests had to be constructed to the same extent that the Great Bear Rainforest had to be constructed. Both the object of BC coastal environmental politics and the group that emerged to protect it were produced (as I will show) through a linked series of processes: a "scientific" ecosystem mapping project, a "discursive" project to collect stories and images of the coast, as well as a "collective" project, woven through the other two, to shift the focus and interest of environmentalists.

The Coastal Temperate Rainforest

A central feature of the GBR campaign was the claim that "one of the largest remaining tracts of ancient coastal temperate rainforest in the world is found in the Great Bear Rainforest on B.C.'s Mainland Coast" (Thomas and Langer 1998). Where did this claim come from? Little evidence of origin accompanies the claim, since it was presented as a statement of fact (cf. Latour 1987). However, it is possible to pick up some of the early traces.

In the early 1990s, Ecotrust and Conservation International engaged in a Coastal Temperate Rain Forest Mapping Project that sought to define the coastal temperate rainforest and place it in its "global context" (Weigand, Mitchell, and Morgan 1992). As they write in the introduction to their 1992 report on the project,

this paper proposes a new biome, a subdivision of the previously acknowledged temperate rain forest type, the coastal temperate rain forest ... The
decision to formally define this forest type grew out of an interest in placing
the distribution and status of coastal temperate rain forests in a global
context. Like the tropical rain forests which have rightly received so much
attention, these forests are an important part of our global heritage. (1)

As this passage makes clear, this project was simultaneously scientific and
political. It involved the identification and specification of a real thing out
there in the world, the coastal temperate rainforest. While it represented
"a new biome," the authors did not invent the coastal temperate rainforest;
rather, it was proposed as a subdivision of a previously acknowledged
reality: the "temperate rain forest type." Nevertheless, the rainforest is a
hybrid of concept and substance: simultaneously form – the subdivision
of a category – and matter – a previously acknowledged reality. At the
same time, identification of the coastal temperate rainforest was the consequence of a "decision." The authors chose to "formally define" this forest
type in order to link it to tropical rainforests that, they note, have "rightly
received so much attention." The political traction of such a linkage is
substantial. One interviewee related a story about an environmentalist's
(Vicky Husband) encounter with a representative of the Council of Forest
Industries (COFI) at the 1992 UN Conference on Environment and
Development:

> [Mike Apsey of] COFI was up there saying, "we've got to protect the
> tropical rainforest, one is the planet, blah, blah, blah." Well, along
> with the crappy things that [the forestry industry is doing] here [in
> British Columbia], right? So he was down there, she runs into him in
> the hallway somewhere, and she made a comment to him, something
> to the effect of, you know, "Canada has a rainforest as well, and one of
> these days people are going to figure that out." And she said, "he just
> went white because he knew what that meant." [Laughter]

The goal of defining the coastal temperate rainforest was not easily
achieved: the authors could neither simply point to the coastal temperate
rainforest that was out there waiting to be discovered nor invent it out of
the blue. Many steps were needed to progressively "load the world into
discourse" (Latour 1999, 96). That is, the authors had to translate the central
and north coasts into the coastal temperate rainforest through a number
of frames and formats. Latour's expression is useful here since it keeps us

from thinking that the authors projected a representation onto material reality; in contrast, material reality was mobilized, enrolled, and shaped into new forms through definitions and devices, thus creating a materially dense representation – one that could be traced back to its source.

The authors first identified the elements with which they would define the coastal temperate rainforest, a difficult task since "within the scientific community there remain[ed] some discussion regarding a global definition of coastal temperate rain forest" (Weigand et al. 1992, 3). This particular forest type was not yet an accepted fact but was still in the process of being produced, including the nuances, differences of opinion, and controversies that go along with such a process. Indeed,

> forest classification schemes within the coastal temperate rain forest zone vary considerably from country to country. Chile and Argentina, for example, classify their forests by geoclimatic parameters at the regional level, and by microsite and habitat at the community level. Tasmanian ecologists distinguish forest types biogeographically, according to altitude and climatic variables. (3)

Given this level of uncertainty and even controversy over the features that define the coastal temperate rainforest, the authors were forced to make a decision. Weigand of Ecotrust proposed the following "working definition" of the coastal temperate rainforest: "areas between 32 and 60 degrees latitude, with the presence of vegetation (if not currently, then originally in a forested condition), with at least 2000 mm (80 in) of annual rainfall" (Weigand et al. 1992, 4). This definition frames and orders data associated with the coastal forests. However, the frame does not simply consist of words, ideas, beliefs, and meanings that "socially construct" the forests. Rather, it is a hybrid frame made up of heterogeneous materials: a political goal of inducing interest in a particular region, a working definition bringing provisional settlement to a scientific controversy spanning several countries, and geographic, botanical, and meteorological specifications. The frame enrols and assembles rain, space, and plant life – which had already taken the form or frame of tables and maps providing information about precipitation, vegetation, forest, and land use. The result is the translation of particular areas of the Earth into a forest type – the coastal temperate rainforest – that were then assembled onto a map to depict their global distribution. In Weigand's judgment, approximately 30 million hectares of coastal temperate rainforest existed before major human alterations. Against this backdrop, the authors highlighted the threatened nature of this forest. While they admit that "the total area of remaining coastal temperate rain forest is unknown," they refer to "researchers [who] believe that 17.3 million hectares (42.7 million acres) or 56% of the total has been logged and converted to non-forest use" (Weigand et al. 1992, 5).

The attempt to formally define a new biome as a subdivision of the previously acknowledged temperate rainforest type was the outcome of practices that mixed (among other elements) working definitions, precipitation, rhetorical devices (maps), and satellite images for the purpose of engaging in public debates about land use. Is the coastal temperate rainforest real or constructed? If we accept the first perspective, then we grant scientific representation privileged access to reality. According to this view, scientists go out into the world (or the laboratory) to "discover" facts that always existed independent of their work to uncover them. Knowledge of natural processes enters the political sphere only after the fact, so to speak, through the work of scientific popularizers and activists who put scientific claims on the political agenda (Hannigan 2006; Kranjc 2002).

In contrast, if we accept the second perspective, then we are suggesting that people can know the world only through social processes of interpretation and that science – rather than escaping from these processes to directly access the world as it is – actively contributes to the production of frameworks of meaning (Irwin 2001). Despite the claims of critics (Dunlap and Catton 1994; Murphy 1994), the latter perspective generally does not hold that there is no reality behind or beyond social constructions, but it does withhold ontological claims altogether in order to focus on epistemological questions (Burningham and Cooper 1999). Thus, notwithstanding their differences, both perspectives entail that mixtures of science and politics occlude access to reality: the first as a form of bias, the second as an inevitable effect of epistemology.

However, a third possibility exists: reality is both constructed and real, indeed real because it is constructed (Latour 1999, 127). In this view, there is no huge gap between representation and reality that is either bridged by an accurate correspondence between word and world or filled with social constructions. Rather, the connection between word and world is made through movement across multiple gaps or what Latour refers to as "circulating reference":

> At every stage, each element belongs to matter by its origin and to form by
> its destination ... We never detect the rupture between things and signs,
> and we never face the imposition of arbitrary and discrete signs on shapeless

and continuous matter. We see only an unbroken series of well-nested elements, each of which plays the role of sign for the previous one and of thing for the succeeding one. (56)

In Latour's terms, classification of the coastal temperate rainforest as a global forest type does indeed refer to British Columbia's coastal forests but not through a correspondence between the concept of coastal temperate rainforest and the coastal forests themselves. If Weigand and others walked (or, more likely, boated) into British Columbia's coastal forests, then they would not have seen, smelled, or touched a coastal temperate rainforest. However, this does not entail that they are greatly biased, merely projecting an unrecognized social representation onto the forests. Rather, as described above, there are intermediary steps linking the word and the world, thus "loading" the coastal forests into the report on the coastal temperate rainforest.

At each step – coming up with a provisional definition; collecting data on precipitation, vegetation, and land cover; estimating original coverage; translating that estimate into a visual depiction on a map – there is a gap that must be crossed. "Previously acknowledged" definitions of temperate rainforests must be sifted through and translated into a provisional definition of the coastal temperate rainforest; this definition must be translated into data; data must be translated into an estimate; the estimate must be translated into a map; the map must be translated into a call to action. At each step, the thing undergoes a transformation but nevertheless refers back to its former self: the map can be turned back into an estimate, an estimate back into raw data, and so on. At the extremes are British Columbia's coastal forests and the concept of the coastal temperate rainforest. However, it is the chain of translations that links them together, the circulation in both directions across the multiple gaps of reference. It is the entire chain – one constructed out of provisional definitions, rhetoric, data, and satellites – that provides the reality of the coastal temperate rainforest and the call for its protection.

Unprotected Watersheds

With the definition of coastal temperate rainforest in place, Ecotrust and Conservation International turned to designing strategies to interest environmental activists in the forest's fate. At the time, most wilderness activists were busy chaining themselves to trees in reactive battles focused on the protection of individual valleys in the south (Stansbury 2000; Wilson

1998). As such, they were unaware of the potential for a proactive, comprehensive conservation vision for the largest remaining intact coastal temperate rainforest to the north. To capture their interest, the environmental organizations joined forces with Earthlife Canada Foundation to commission a report entitled *Coastal Watersheds: An Inventory of Watersheds in the Coastal Temperate Forests of British Columbia* (Moore 1991). In the preface to the report, a well-known BC environmentalist (John Broadhead) wrote that, "to date, British Columbia has confronted the issue [of wilderness conservation] on a piecemeal basis ... watershed by watershed ... jobs versus the environment and 'the last unlogged watershed.' This paper is provided for those who are calling for a different approach – for a comprehensive land use strategy" (2).

To help facilitate a new direction and focus, the author of the report (Keith Moore) reversed the direction between world and words by loading discourse into the world. Starting with the abstract global category of the temperate rainforest, he applied a series of conceptual, physical, and graphical devices to identify specific spaces where the rainforest could be located. Essentially, this was a mapping exercise; however, its primary goal was to articulate particular biophysical spaces with the interests of environmentalists, thereby convincing them that they could best achieve their aims by shifting their focus northward.

First, Moore identified a unit of measurement that resonated with environmentalists' current frame of reference: the watershed. As he noted in his introduction, "in recent years, many of the conservation efforts in the coastal temperate forests of British Columbia have focused on the need to preserve entire, intact watersheds" (1991, 4). This statement articulated the watershed with the "coastal temperate forests," thereby simultaneously recognizing environmentalists' interests and shifting their focus "away from the 'last unlogged watershed' syndrome" (4). Second, Moore specified environmentalists' interests by drawing on public conservation groups, parks system planners, researchers in biological processes, and conservation professionals to argue that watersheds are representative of their ecosystems, are large enough to prevent fragmentation of wildlife habitat, and can preserve recreational and wilderness values (4).

To identify watersheds, Moore used the BC Ministry of Environment's Watershed Coding System as well as existing maps that identified watersheds on Vancouver Island and the Queen Charlotte Islands. The goal was to identify watersheds over 5,000 hectares in size, a number somewhat arbitrarily chosen but matching the Wilderness Advisory Committee's suggestion that 5,000 hectares are "the minimum appropriate size for an area to be considered wilderness" (Moore 1991, 4). Thus, instead of beginning with the "global context," as did Ecotrust, Moore began with the local by drawing on systems and classifications made in British Columbia, identifying watersheds, and working back to the larger context. Through these methods, he identified over 600 watersheds that possibly exceeded 5,000 hectares. By drawing them on maps and measuring their areas with a planimeter – an instrument that measures the area of an arbitrary two-dimensional shape – he identified 354 watersheds over 5,000 hectares in size (a small number were determined from other sources).

Moore then crosscut these watersheds with information about development status and protected status. With respect to development status, he conducted interviews with Ministry of Forests staff to determine whether and to what extent logging activity had taken place within each watershed. He then verified these interviews with air photos and detailed forest cover maps. Where evidence of limited industrial activity (logging roads, powerlines, pipelines, mining, settlements) was found, Moore measured the extent on the photos and maps. With this information, he defined watersheds as "pristine" (having virtually no – i.e., less than five hectares – evidence of industrial activities), "modified" (having less than 2 percent of the total area affected by industrial activities), and "developed" (having more than 2 percent of the total area affected by industrial activities). With respect to protected status, he drew the boundaries of protected areas on his maps to determine whether and the extent to which watersheds were encompassed by protected area boundaries.

The result was a report, map, and table that identified watersheds larger than 5,000 hectares that included information on development status and protected status. The report translated the coastal forest into 354 watersheds, 236 (67 percent) of which were developed and 118 (33 percent) of which were either pristine (72 or 20 percent) or modified (46 or 13 percent). Of the 354 watersheds, only nine were fully protected, and only six of them were pristine (three were modified). In other words (if modified areas can be considered conservation opportunities because of the limited extent of industrial impact), Moore's report translated the coastal forests into over 100 conservation opportunities that could be identified as dots on a map. Most of the conservation opportunities existed north of Vancouver Island, where, in comparison with the south coast, "many more undeveloped primary watersheds remain" (Moore 1991, 19). Of 174 watersheds in the southern portion of British Columbia, only fourteen were pristine or modified. In contrast, of 180 watersheds on the central and northern coasts, 104 were pristine or modified.

These maps presented the BC environmental movement – used to fighting over individual watersheds – with a veritable smorgasbord of conservation opportunities. By comparing the south coast map with the mid- and north coast map, environmentalists were able to see at a glance that, by far, greater conservation opportunities existed to the north than to the south. Moreover, an essay by Ecotrust and Conservation International (Beebe and Wolf 1991, 37) linked these individual conservation opportunities back into the "global context" of the coastal temperate rainforest: "While the biota and productivity values in these watersheds are unique and in some cases exceptional, their ecosystem characteristics are nonetheless similar to the coastal forests of Chile, southern Norway, and Tasmania." These ecosystem characteristics, of course, are those that qualify the BC coastal watersheds as belonging to the coastal temperate rainforest. Their essay, entitled "The Coastal Temperate Rain Forest: An Ecosystem Management Perspective," offered descriptions of this forest type's rarity, threatened status, and remaining extent. On this basis, Beebe and Wolf concluded that "British Columbia occupies a position of central, indeed global importance":

> Here the coastal temperate forest zone blankets 6.5 million hectares over the full length of the coastline. It contains a wide variety of local forest types within the Coastal Western Hemlock and Coastal Douglas fir biogeoclimatic zones. And in marked contrast to the US, significant opportunities still remain to protect large, unlogged and highly productive coastal watersheds ... These [watersheds] represent an important conservation opportunity – not just for BC and Canada, but for the world as a whole. (37)

A great deal of work went into translating the coastal temperate rainforest into terms that might interest activists. Was it successful? The Western Canada Wilderness Committee was one of the first to indicate interest in the report. The committee used one of its "educational reports" (WCWC 1992) to promote the idea of the BC coastal temperate rainforest and its watersheds to a wider audience:

> When most people think about rainforests, they imagine steamy hot tropical jungles of South and Central America, Asia and Africa. But rainforests – lush forests that grow where precipitation is at least 2000 mm (over 6 feet) and is spread out relatively evenly over most of the year, are also found in

temperate regions of the world. Temperate rainforests grow along a thin band of land where moist ocean air collides with coastal mountains.

The report repeats many of the points made in Beebe and Wolf's (1991) essay and provides details on Moore's (1991) report, including advice on how to read his tables. The report notes a few characteristics of the temperate rainforest, its rarity as a global forest type, its greatly diminished extent, and its excellent conservation opportunity in British Columbia: "Only one third of BC's primary temperate watersheds are still wild. We have a responsibility to all inhabitants of this planet, present and future, to set aside self-sustaining areas of temperate rainforest as wilderness, forever."

Within this wide-angle view, the report then moves on to provide details on opportunities to preserve particular coastal watersheds. It notes that, "in the southern-most regions of the coast, we have already lost the chance to protect whole, undeveloped watersheds over 5,000 ha in size. Only fragmented watersheds remain" (WCWC 1992). In contrast,

> most of the remaining undeveloped watersheds in coastal BC are located in the North Coast region. Here there is the opportunity to create a huge protected area which extends from the coastal divide, and Tweedsmuir Park, all the way south to Fiordland Recreation Area (which must be upgraded to class A park) and the ocean.

The goal of protecting the central and north coasts' pristine watersheds brought together international environmental organizations (Conservation International and Ecotrust), with their focus on a "global" forest type, and a local grassroots environmental group, with its focus on specific, local watersheds, which, nevertheless, are of interest to the entire planet. Is the effort global or local? Neither; rather, there is a single chain connecting all of the actors. If we look at any one link in the chain – Moore's planimeter, Weigand's working definition, the Ministry of Forests's biogeoclimatic classification system, Broadhead's appeal, or the Western Canada Wilderness Committee's educational report – we do not find global or local, just a link in the chain. Start removing links, and the global context of the coastal temperate rainforest becomes just an idea not connected to anybody, while the Western Canada Wilderness Committee's members continue to focus on the "last unlogged watersheds" of the southern coast. But link them together, and local things in many locations start to become connected with one another.

Stories and Images

If a central claim about British Columbia's central and north coasts was that they comprised a coastal temperate rainforest, another was that this forest was full of beauty and life. It was not simply a stockpile of resources – a "timber supply area" – but also contained "lush rainforest valleys [that] are home to some of the oldest and biggest trees on earth and provide critical refuge for grizzly bears, salmon and a rare snow-white variation of the black bear called the 'Kermode' or 'Spirit' bear" (Greenpeace 1997c). As noted by one environmentalist, one of the most significant victories was getting people to recognize the central and north coasts not as a timber supply area but as the Great Bear Rainforest. Where did *this* claim come from?

Sociologists tend to treat scientific and cultural claims separately (Callon 1986). Associated with this tendency is the view that science accesses the facts of nature – there whether we like them or not – while culture freely constructs meanings and symbols. While sociological analyses of scientific claims are thereby generally restricted to their social contexts – analyzing how economic, political, and ideological forces influence choice of research topic, for example, while leaving the content of the research unexamined – no such constraints exist for the study of culture. Sociologists are free to study the "cultural logic," or the "sets of institutionalized beliefs, practices and mythologies" (Rossiter 2004, 141), behind environmentalists' claims about nature. According to this perspective, we could analyze Ian and Karen McAllister's 1997 coffee table book *The Great Bear Rainforest,* laced as it is with gorgeous photographs and evocative prose, for the ways in which it visually and discursively constructs the Great Bear Rainforest as a set of meanings imposed onto the landscape. For example, the McAllisters write that

we never tire of watching [grizzly bears], because each bear has a unique personality and because their relationship with the forest is so uncanny. At first the bears' massive bulk and heavy armament seem out of place in an environment so soft and spongelike, but the grace with which the huge creatures disport themselves among all this fragile complexity is a virtuoso performance that we can't stop applauding. Sometimes on busy bear trails we find clumps of untouched wildflowers we swear they must be stepping around deliberately. Elsewhere, bears searching for root plants have ripped up estuary soils like bulldozers – which couldn't be better for the estuary. It is this multi-faceted relationship between the bear and the forest that we have found our most rewarding study, and if we dwell on it, it is because we find it the most profound symbol of what this ancient ecosystem is all about. (25-26)

We do not have to search long to find the primary symbol that the McAllisters are constructing: grizzly bears represent the "ancient ecosystem." They are ideal symbols since we can relate to them (they are full of personality), admire them (they are beautiful, graceful performers), and respect them (they carry out important roles in the ecosystem). Moreover, the bears are represented as managers and stewards of the rainforest's ecological integrity. Strong and powerful, they are nevertheless gentle when they need to protect the rainforest's "fragile complexity," going so far (perhaps) as "deliberately" stepping around "untouched wildflowers." Delicate and graceful, the bears nevertheless unleash their massive power when appropriate, as when they contribute to the health of estuaries by digging them up "like bulldozers." The great bear, loaded with symbols and meanings, is put forward by the McAllisters as the ideal representative of the rainforest.

In this representation, the word seems quite removed from the world. It appears that the gap is crossed by a projection, an interpretation wherein the forests are socially constructed as the Great Bear Rainforest. Yet how is this representation produced? Is it merely the product of visual and discursive rhetoric? Where did these pictures and words come from? Immediately below the McAllisters' identification of bears as the "most profound" symbol of the rainforest is an excerpt from Ian's field notes, accompanied by a full-page picture of a bear gazing into the eyes of the reader.

IAN'S JOURNAL: I should have realized that the sudden flurry of gurglings and throaty cracks from the ravens above me meant that there were more life forms about than just me and the birds. Suddenly the devil's club and salmonberry bushes began to shake and I knew that within seconds huge claws would be digging into the mud of the well-worn bear trail where my gumboots were currently planted. I backed off to the side about twenty feet, trying to decide whether to run, yell, play dead or pray to God, and finally chose, out of confusion mixed with curiosity and fascination, to do nothing. I sank deep into the moss of an old spruce stump – bear spray in hand – and just watched as the big bear lumbered down the trail, nose up, and stopped in mid-stride right in front of me. We stared at each other across the sword ferns. Salmon blood stained his mouth and he seemed well fed.

He did not seem alarmed at my presence. The look in his eyes when they met mine was one of gentleness, almost sentience ... Then the 225-kilogram bear lowered his head and passed on without even snapping a twig, as beautiful as anything I have seen. (McAllister and McAllister 1997, 26)

This excerpt places the reader on the edge of his or her seat. The excitement of imminent danger – foreshadowed by images of shaking bushes, claws, "sword" ferns, and the blood-stained mouth of a big grizzly bear – draws the reader into the scene and its visceral experience. It also serves to highlight the bravery and humanity of Ian McAllister. He willingly puts himself into dangerous situations in which, like us if we were in his position, he does not know "whether to run, yell, play dead or pray to God." He does so to bring us the stories and experiences of a place that we would otherwise never see, a place that he selflessly is working so hard to protect. The tension set up in his narrative is resolved in a pleasantly unexpected manner. The grizzly bear is not fierce but gentle, calm, and beautiful. McAllister has nothing to fear: the bear moves on, gracefully as ever, a gentle giant who does not even snap a twig, let alone wantonly disembowel a human. Moreover, the encounter is not one of violence but one of connection, a meeting of eyes and, perhaps, minds – a meeting that the reader is invited to make by gazing into the eyes of the photographed bear that gazes back.

All of these discursive effects of McAllister's narrative and accompanying photograph are worth analyzing. These elements construct a particular set of meanings and symbolic connections between humans and bears, which in turn are constructed as the gentle giant representatives of the rainforest. However, it is worth noting another feature of the text: it is a journal entry. It thereby refers back to a different time and place. Similarly, the photograph obviously came from somewhere. If we look closely, we can notice that the background in the photo consists of water, not forest. Additionally, given that McAllister was too busy squeezing himself into a stump in fear for his life to snap a photo of his would-be killer, this shot is obviously of a different bear. Yet it is assembled in the text in support of his story. Moreover, other elements, from different times and places, also help to construct the great bear as a representative of the rainforest. For example, the McAllisters invoke claims from the science of conservation biology that grizzly bears serve as an *umbrella species* for ecosystems:

We can look at healthy grizzly populations and have confidence that the integrity of the coastal ecosystem is intact and that the 230 bird species,

68 mammals, and thousands of insects and microorganisms that make their home in the old-growth forests are also healthy. If the grizzly numbers start to go down, we can be sure that those other less visible values are declining too. This is reason enough to focus worldwide attention on these bears. (McAllister and McAllister 1997, 25)

The coffee table book is comprised of images, metaphors, and symbols, but these elements are assembled from different times and places in order to construct these representations. Where did these images and stories come from?[1] If we trace the histories of these objects and the representations that they create, we can identify the links in the chain connecting the coastal forests with the representation Great Bear Rainforest – just as I did for the coastal temperate rainforest. These two representations – one seemingly scientific and the other seemingly cultural – do not have to be analyzed in separate ways but can be considered symmetrically (Callon 1986). They are both black boxes that can be opened up if we attend to the practices through which they were assembled.

In fact, when we attend to practice, we find that the scientific chain (made up of a diverse mixture of data, provisional definitions, instruments, and rhetoric) is directly connected to the cultural chain (which, as I describe below, is similarly made up of a mixture of science and politics). The McAllisters' interest in the central and north coasts, like that of the Western Canada Wilderness Committee, was prompted by Moore's watershed inventory. As Ian McAllister mentioned in an interview,

> while a lot of the Vancouver Island stuff was going on in 1989, Keith Moore was contacted by Conservation International and Earthlife Canada and, I think, Ecotrust to do a watershed inventory of the entire BC coast. He published that report about then, and it basically was the catalyst for our work up on the central and north coast of BC because it showed there was maybe half a dozen intact primary rainforest river valleys over 5,000 hectares in size on the island, and yet, on the central/north coast it was just massive clusters of dots on the map showing many, many intact river systems, [but] nobody was working up there at that time.

The McAllisters took up the relay offered by Conservation International and Ecotrust's coastal temperate rainforest by translating Moore's watersheds into stories and images. This was not simply a matter of inventing symbols and metaphors but also – as with the coastal temperate rainforest representation – involved the hard work of loading the world back into discourse (Latour 1999). Indeed, this work involved a fair amount of lay science.

As they recount in their book, the McAllisters (1997, 15) began to collect "as much information as we could about every dot on the map, scouting provincial and federal government offices and libraries. The information barely filled a shoebox." In response, they decided to go out and collect information directly from the coastal forests. In an interview, Ian recounted that

> we didn't know what was up there, and it took a number of years
> just to do the basic baseline inventory and research. And I mean basic
> – like, we were just running from valley to valley, looking at estuaries,
> trying to understand the status of salmon and bears, trying to under-
> stand the basic forest cover, just having the first real look from the
> outside world of these river systems.

It is one thing to take the coast in at a glance by referring to a map produced by Weigand or Moore, but to go back to the territory to which these maps refer and fill in the dots is another. The same remoteness and ruggedness of the area that had thus far prevented large-scale forestry operations made it difficult to canvass the coast for conservation purposes. The sheer size of the coastline led to technical innovations by the McAllisters, who first accessed the region by boat, as Ian noted in an interview:

> We're talking over 10,000 miles of coastline. [We were] going up and
> down these fiords and whatnot, and your boat might only go seven, eight
> knots, and you can only cover so much ground in a day, so I spent a lot
> of time with volunteer pilots, flying up and down valleys. Like old World
> War II fighter pilots, like Mike Humphries ... We would spend, literally,
> weeks and weeks in the air. Day after day, landing in Bella Coola, and
> Prince Rupert, and Kitimat, and all these places, with a video camera on
> the wing. And I had the door off taking pictures. [We were] going up
> and down the river systems and then going back and cataloguing it and
> beginning to put together a piece. But the more and more we did that,
> the more we realized ... how extensive this coastline was.

When the McAllisters visited the coast physically rather than through mediation on Moore's map, the "massive" and "extensive coastline" was impossible to see synoptically. If they were to take in more than a tiny fragment of the forest at a time, they had to work to displace their perspective (Latour 1999, 66). To do so, they enlisted the skills of a pilot trained for war, the capabilities of a small aircraft, and the technology of video and still photographs. This displacement is not different in kind from the dislocation of perspective achieved by Conservation International and Ecotrust via their global information system technology or by Moore via his planimeter. Rather, all three parties were forced to rely on devices to gain new perspectives on the coast, which, in their absence, takes on the aspect of a "delightfully tangled up territory" (McAllister and McAllister 1997, 44). For their part, the McAllisters were able to convert the coastline into a portable format that could be reviewed at any time away from the coastline itself. By means of photographs, they could associate dots on Moore's map with visual depictions of individual valleys. By means of video, they could fast-forward, rewind, and pause on certain images of the coastline as they catalogued its watersheds.

As Ian mentioned in an interview, they spent the next five years sailing up and down the coast, "ground-truthing" the rough information that they had collected from the air. The McAllisters populated Moore's watersheds with waterways, salmon streams, estuaries, plants and trees, and wolf and bear populations. Perhaps even more importantly, they collected stories and photographs. Their coffee table book is full of these stories and images, which take the form of narratives, journal excerpts, and glossy full-page colour photographs. By the time readers reach the end of the book, having virtually travelled with the McAllisters along the entire coastline, they encounter a map listing the coast's "endangered intact watersheds," one not much different from Moore's. However, in this case, each dot has been filled in with stories and gorgeous photographs.

Having taken over the relay offered by Conservation International and Ecotrust, the McAllisters (and their environmental group, the Raincoast Conservation Society) worked to interest other BC environmentalists in the region. According to Ian,

it was almost surreal for us to be sailing quietly up on the central and north coast [along] these vast intact, unprotected, and threatened river valleys day after day and then reading or listening to the news [about] the massive blockades and the huge displays of civil disobedience happening in Clayoquot Sound. In the back of our minds, we're wondering, "when are people going to pay attention to this coast?" It took a few years for sure.

Thus, while the coffee table book was directed toward a general audience who might be induced to support the aims of an environmental campaign, the McAllisters' first task was to help "usher in" such a campaign. Largely, this involved deploying the same images and stories that would be compiled in the book. As Ian recounted in an interview, "a lot of our earlier work was really just as a messenger, getting those tools [out] – those video and still images and stories – and introducing people to First Nations and just trying to usher in a campaign." As Ian noted, they took the information that they collected about the area to local, national, and international environmental organizations: "We were going to Europe each winter, and we were travelling around Canada and the United States, banging on doors and trying to get people engaged in the issues and the campaigns."

This translation is continuous with the previous two and draws together material, symbolic, and collective elements. The symbol of the great bear was materially and painstakingly produced over five years of "inventory and research," refining the construction of the object of environmental concern to the same extent as it reworked the subject of environmental concern.

Assembling a Panorama of the Coastal Forests

Three important translations of British Columbia's coastal forests took place between 1990 and 1996. The place was scaled up into a coastal temperate rainforest located within a global distribution, drilled down into an inventory of unprotected watersheds, and filled out with experiences, stories, and symbols. While some aspects of these translations appeared to be purely scientific and others to be purely discursive, all of the translations blended material, discursive, and collective elements. Moreover, they were connected together in a continuous chain. Rather than a non-human reality "out there" that scientists discovered or that environmentalists (mis)represented, the coastal forests were mobilized by a variety of devices and techniques in order to influence how people connect with them. Each translation created a particular depiction of the forests, connecting them through a single chain.

However, these depictions were not assembled into one synoptic, total view of the forests until the Sierra Club produced a composite map of the region. In 1996, it released a satellite map of coastal British Columbia entitled Canada's Rainforest – Worth Saving. The map is an aesthetically striking work of art, as captivating, in its own way, as the McAllisters' photographs. Rich aquamarines, forest greens, and unearthy yellows draw the viewer into the glossy illustration, offering a unique view of a unique place. This is Canada's rainforest, large enough to extend along the entire West Coast but tiny – and therefore precious – when considered in relation to the size of the continent. A small panel of complementary photographs tells the larger story depicted on the map. A cedar tree so large that we can see only its trunk, salmon eggs viewed so closely that we cannot fail to recognize their importance, a grizzly bear so large that it fills the frame, and a First Nations carving so old that it appears to be part of nature itself – these representatives suggest what is "worth saving" in this rainforest. There are no people in these photographs, only plants and animals.

These elements of the Sierra Club map thus represent the coastal forests in a particular way, and I have given a particularly social constructionist reading of this representation. But this is a hybrid map. Other elements resist reading it as a purely human construction. In the text describing the "rare, unique, and threatened" status of the rainforest, we once more encounter the claim produced by Conservation International and Ecotrust's rainforest mapping project: the rainforest covers "just a fifth of one percent of the earth's land surface," with British Columbia's portion representing "almost one quarter of all that is left in the world" (Sierra Club of BC 1996). This scientific-political "factish," to use Latour's (1999, 274) term for facts that have gone through traceable processes of fabrication, does its intended work by entailing that "here we have one of the best chances to conserve these wild and ancient rainforests, along with the grizzly bear, salmon and countless species that depend on old growth for their survival" (Sierra Club of BC 1996).

Other features of the map refer to things that exceed a purely discursive reading. The most important features, of course, are the yellow and green areas. They are aesthetically striking, but they also refer to things beyond the map itself. Yellow areas refer to areas that have been "logged," while green areas refer to the "remaining ancient forest." The text accompanying the chart tells us that "more than half [53.1 percent] of B.C.'s coastal rainforest is gone." We might conclude that the situation is good because we still have about 50 percent of the remaining forest, but our feeling of comfort is quickly taken from us with the knowledge that only a "thin sliver is protected for our children," while what remains faces an unrelenting, violent onslaught, since "virtually all pristine valleys will have logging roads punched into them in the next two decades" (Sierra Club of BC 1996). Are these facts and figures simply conjured up for rhetorical purposes? Are they simply transparent depictions of realities discovered by scientists?

What about the view from space? Surely, this seemingly objective view is not what we would see if we were aboard the orbiting satellite.

The Sierra Club map is the product of a chain of circulating reference, just like Conservation International and Ecotrust's coastal temperate rainforest and the McAllisters' photographs and stories. Each element assembled in the map, from the colours to the photographs to the pie chart, has a history.[2] Indeed, the mapping project itself has a history: it was the extension of an earlier mapping project covering Vancouver Island. As recounted by Braun (2002, 215), the Sierra Club produced two maps of Vancouver Island in the early 1990s that compared the extent of forest cover in 1954 with that in 1990. The maps were presented as satellite images, seemingly objective snapshots of the island in two different time periods. The purpose of the maps was to visually demonstrate the extent of "the disappearing forest" on Vancouver Island (reproduced in Braun on 215). Yet, according to Braun, the images were not simple snapshots from space: they were the outcomes of a great deal of work. The images were computer generated, with Landsat imagery (satellite photographs) forming only one source of information for the final products. Other resources included forest inventories produced by the Ministry of Forests, "vegetation zone" categories produced by biogeographers and represented in maps of biogeoclimatic units, and colour schemes introduced by cartographers. These sources were digitally combined with one another to produce the final image. Thus, according to Braun,

> the images combined and translated material from multiple sources (satellite photographs, biogeoclimatic maps, forest inventories, air photographs), mixed these with the skills of technicians (photographers, computer programmers, cartographers), relied on the competencies of various instruments (computers, software, satellite technologies, cameras, printers), and drew on a set of guiding metaphors and concepts from sciences such as ecology. (223)

The result of this hard work was a new actor: "Reproduced in pamphlets, hung on walls, shown at rallies, and reproduced in the pages of newspapers and magazines, it [the map] helped to fuel a global campaign to save the 'ancient rainforests' of Vancouver Island" (Braun 2002, 222). Similarly, the Sierra Club's Canada's Rainforest map became an important actor, inasmuch as it helped to "usher in" a campaign for British Columbia's central and north coasts. The map served to draw environmental activists' attention to the coastal forests lying north of their most recent battles. As the map made apparent, wilderness advocates had previously focused their efforts on protecting tiny pockets of green in an expanding sea of yellow in the southern half of the province. Their successes were thus best viewed as small green wins in a wider yellow failure. In contrast, the map directed environmentalists' attention to an area where it would be more effective: the north. According to the Sierra Club (2008), the map

> showed the extent of rainforest destruction on Vancouver Island, along B.C.'s south coast and its gradual extension northwards up the coast. It also highlighted the extensive intact areas that could still be saved in the Central and North Coast. For the first time, British Columbians could clearly see how much of the rainforest was gone, and what remained.

Indeed, this was the first time that viewers could "see" the rainforest and its extent in coastal British Columbia. The map presented a panoramic view of the central and north coasts, one that situated them in relation to Canada, the world, future generations, forestry, animals, and the concerned viewer. But, as described above, this was not an unmediated, objective vision, nor was it merely a representation with no connection to the reality beyond the text. The visual depiction was an achievement produced through the assemblage – through chains of translations – of many different types of things, thus offering viewers a synoptic "god's-eye view" of forest cover data, ecological classifications, historical and contemporary logging practices, future generations, "ancient" metaphors, trees, bears, salmon, and geography. Much work went into the production of a map reproducible on a single, and thus highly portable, piece of paper. This composite but single actor-network helped environmentalists to "see" where they should focus their efforts.

A panorama is a kind of projection, a representation of a world or state of affairs. It provides a total view. It does not provide a transparent representation of the world as it is. But this is not to say that it is merely socially constructed. Rather, as I have detailed in this chapter, the construction of a panorama is a material undertaking as much as it is a discursive one. Environmental politics applies to the assemblage of such heterogeneous networks. Only if we ignore all the hard work in constructing this panorama can we conceive of a material reality "out there" in which politics is engaged "in here." Rather, environmental politics involves the chaining of elements such as rain, vegetation, watersheds, experiences, stories, and people into a new quasi-object – Canada's rainforest – and a new quasi-subject[3] – the viewer who believes that it is worth saving. Moreover, the point of constructing such panoramas is not to transparently depict the world as it is but to induce others to act in particular ways. It becomes a practical means of creating new associations. Thus, care must be taken in the representation of the panoramas themselves – if they are to induce interest, then they must be made interesting.

The Sierra Club's satellite map is visually compelling, yet what viewers could see as obvious was still rather formless, as one environmentalist noted: "We used to call it the 'Big Green Blob' before it was called the 'Great Bear Rainforest.' I mean, we didn't call it that publicly, but that's what we called it in meetings." The Big Green Blob was open ended and ill defined. Satellites, land-use data, mapping technologies, conservation biology, attempts to influence the focus of the environmental movement – all of these things came together to create an open-ended thing. In Latour's (2004, 247) terms, the "blob" was little more than a "proposition," or an association of humans and non-humans, before it became recognized and instituted in a collective.[4] At this stage, the possibilities for this ill-defined thing were still open ended.

However, the forms of thought that make up the *modern constitution* – the practices that simultaneously proliferate hybrids of humans and non-humans and conceptually separate them into society and nature (Latour 1993) – were at play, and, while environmentalists and others worked to create this new hybrid network, they sought to prematurely purify it into non-human nature without proper debate, or what Latour refers to as "due process." Ecotrust and Conservation International worked to produce a new forest type – not to connect the coastal forests more intimately with people but to protect them *from* people. The McAllisters worked to populate the coastal watersheds with images and stories to argue for their *preservation*. The Western Canada Wilderness Committee popularized Moore's watershed inventory and the concept of the coastal temperate rainforest to promote the idea of creating a giant park *off limits* to development. The Sierra Club produced its map to help people see that Canada has a rainforest worth *saving*. Indeed, while the processes involved in the above endeavours associated heterogeneous materials in novel for-mations, these realities were purified to present a wilderness that had to be protected from people.

These practices of purification were evident in the first name given for this Big Green Blob: Ian McAllister referred to it as the Great Bear Wilderness. The term "wilderness," as numerous scholars have pointed out (e.g., Cronon 1996), presents a view of nature as non-human. However, this purification was resisted even at this stage. As McAllister noted, if you look at our original conservation [proposal] for the coast, it was called the Great Bear Wilderness, but we actually got a fair amount of push back from First Nations. You know, you read the Webster's dictionary, and its definition of "wilderness" is actually quite clear, it says that it's void of humans, right?

First Nations, as I indicate in Chapter 3, resisted definitions of the term "wilderness" that excluded their cultural, jurisdictional, and economic interests, "so it [the name] got changed to the Great Bear Rainforest." The name change took place at a meeting between the McAllisters and a Greenpeace representative in 1996:

I still have distinct memories of Karen [McAllister], Ian McAllister and myself [Tzeporah Berman] sitting in a restaurant in San Francisco in 1996 writing on a paper tablecloth – Great Bear Wilderness? Raincoast Wilderness? Northern Rainforest? Coastal Rainforest Wilderness? And the moment when we wrote Great Bear Rainforest, we all knew immediately that was it. And we were damn sure that Great Bear Rainforest was going to solicit more concern than the "mid coast timber supply area," which is what the region was known to us up until we launched the campaign. (Berman 2006a)

In one sense, the name was "dreamed up" by three people sitting in a restaurant. However, the words chosen were not empty signifiers that could be freely loaded with a "cultural logic." Rather, the words were already dense with signification.

The term "great bear" refers to the "profound symbol" of the grizzly bear, which, as the McAllisters (1997) note in their book, is a natural representative of the forests due both to its gentle yet industrious role in their functioning and to its ability to function as an *umbrella species* within the science of conservation biology. However, the term serves as an umbrella of its own, encompassing not only grizzlies but also the Kermode or "spirit bear," for which the most significant conservation proposal in the region (the Spirit Bear Conservancy) existed at the time of the campaign. Both bears were loaded into the name – not only as discursive symbols but also as representatives of ecosystem integrity and as an existing conservation proposal. Nonetheless, as "charismatic megafauna" (Leader-Williams and Dublin 2000), they served well as "poster icons" (McCrory 2003) for the campaign. The term "rainforest," as analyzed above, is simultaneously scientific and political. Linking these two terms together, the name Great

Bear Rainforest is at once rich with meaning, dense with reference, and the product of relations of power.

This gave the region a particular kind of figuration, which gave it a personality in its own right (Latour 2005b). As one newspaper commentator noted, "a nondescript and emotionally neutral region of British Columbia known as the central and north coast timber supply area entered the public's imagination as a personality worthy of ecological recognition" (Gigg 2006). Environmentalists' interventions transformed the central and north coasts into a new ecological reality, one that would be potentially of interest to others. The Great Bear Rainforest presented a panoramic vision of the coastal forests, a total view that connected the forests to the globe, to animals, to future generations, and to viewers who agreed that it was worth saving. It presented a vision of the future wherein these relations would be realized; thus, while it did not transparently depict the world as it is, it usefully previewed the world to come (Latour 2005b, 189). The protection of Canada's rainforest could not happen in the panorama itself since it remained only a picture of what was to be achieved. More work – and more translations – were required to achieve that end. The next steps were to articulate the GBR in a manner that would enable it to be "recognized" in a specifically "ecological" way and to introduce this "personality" into wider networks in order to solicit concern and enrol other groups in the project of recognizing the GBR.

2

Grizzlies Growl at the International Market

Circulating a Panorama of the Great Bear Rainforest

Once environmentalists had redefined the problem to which BC land-use policy ought to respond, they set out to build a network of support. Doing so involved a process of interesting various groups in the issue or defining their interests in such a way that they could only be met by solving the problem that environmentalists had proposed. More precisely, environmentalists engaged in a process of *interessement* (Callon 1986), positioning themselves between key actors and others who would define their interests differently. The broader wilderness preservation movement would be convinced to shift its focus from threatened individual valleys in the southern portion of the province to the huge area to the north. Representation of the forests would shift from economic to biological criteria. The international market for BC forest products would be persuaded to avoid making purchases unless certain conditions were met. The coastal BC forest companies, in turn, would switch focus from fighting against environmentalists to working with them to preserve ecological values in the region, while environmentalists would switch focus from outright preservation to the reform of forestry practices.

At each place of intervention, various resources were deployed to translate the interests and identities of key actors, bringing them into line with the problem as environmentalists defined it. However, while this process brought together a heterogeneous network of elements, at this stage tension between the desire to purify elements into the conceptual containers of nature and society, on the one hand, and the desire to develop new categories inclusive of the heterogeneity, on the other, persisted. It was not until the various actors began to negotiate their roles in the network (see Chapter 3) that the process shifted more squarely from one of purification to one of composition.

Forming the Canadian Rainforest Network

By 1996, several environmental organizations had become interested in British Columbia's central and north coasts: the McAllisters' Raincoast Conservation Society, the BC Chapter of the Sierra Club, Greenpeace (which had recently established its Ancient Forests Campaign headquarters in Vancouver), the Western Canada Wilderness Committee, and McCrory's Valhalla Wilderness Society. Other groups also became interested in the region. For example, the Forest Action Network (a grassroots, direct action group) established an office in Bella Coola, the heart of the central coast, to support the Nuxalk First Nation in its 1995 blockades of the BC logging company International Forest Products (Interfor) on nearby King Island. However, if a concerted campaign to protect the GBR was to take place, then these different groups needed to be brought together.

Interestingly enough, these groups were united not only by their desire to protect the central and north coasts but also by the mediation of personal growth and spirituality. In 1996, BC Wild convened an "activist training program" consisting of a number of workshops at the Hollyhock Centre focused on helping activists in the wilderness preservation movement to deal with burnout. According to an environmentalist involved in convening these workshops, the Hollyhock Centre is "a personal development retreat centre, basically, like that's kind of what it does. It's all about building personal mastery and personal consciousness, and it's spiritual." While the goal of the workshops was to help activists who were "just flaming and burning [out] all over the place," they originally produced a "huge culture clash" since, in the view of this environmentalist, most activists were "basically about 'get out there in the world and fucking save the planet, and we could care less about crystal fucking, that's not what it's about.'" However, the workshops were eventually able to induce a transformation in the activists: "We're kind of doing this meshing of the spiritual level with the activism piece, and gradually it's getting less and less hard to sell that message internally in the movement." The message was one of "compassion, and [it focused] on the idea of a larger unifying force and all of those kinds of things." Moreover, the workshops provided a venue in which the different groups could develop a common approach to their coastal work: "The group of people who were working on this particular campaign are not only coming here for training, but then they're also having strategy sessions here, and they're starting to do a bunch of work here, just around idea development."

An alliance of twenty small and large, Canadian and American, and radical and moderate groups emerged out of these meetings and was termed the Canadian Rainforest Network. Thus, the original goal of Conservation International and Ecotrust to shift the focus of the BC wilderness preservation movement away from the valley-by-valley struggles characteristic of the "last unlogged watershed syndrome" was largely successful. As noted by the Coastal Rainforest Network coordinator Jill Thomas,

> the idea of doing a valley-by-valley fight on the mainland coast is impossible to contemplate ... There are 60 valleys. But it's time to move beyond that anyway. When we fight valley-by-valley we end up with fragmented valleys here, there and everywhere. This is quite a major paradigm shift for the environmental movement. (cited in Hamilton 1996)

However, the groups differed in their goals, creating tension between the original vision for a giant park and a new, evolving alternative vision for the coastal forests. Some argued that "the whole thing should be protected" (Hamilton 1996), while others focused on protecting some areas while recognizing that "there have to be economic opportunities" (Luke 1996). As one environmentalist whom I interviewed noted,

> the Canadian Rainforest Network was the "who's who" of everybody, and it was like sixteen or eighteen groups of people who were all working up and down the coast. And it was hell, it was like every megalomaniac you've ever met or understood in the world, they were all in the room, and they all had their own ideas about what had to happen, and the spectrum went from the complete idealist who said "reject it all, not a single other tree can come down," to the people who were going "okay, we've got to phase out clear cutting gradually, and now we'll protect some of it." And you know – the incrementalists versus the idealists – and that tension was just palpable in the room, and we spent most of our time fighting.

Latour (1991, 105) notes that "a statement ... is in the hands of others." In other words, a statement, which can refer to "a word, sometimes to a sentence, sometimes to an object, sometimes to an apparatus, and sometimes to an institution" (151), travels through a chain of speakers, each of whom transforms the statement in some way before passing it along. Conservation International and Ecotrust said *coastal temperate rainforest,* Moore said over *100 unprotected watersheds,* the Western Canada Wilderness Committee said *huge park,* the McAllisters and Berman said *Great Bear Rainforest,* Hollyhock said *compassion,* and now the Coastal Rainforest Network was saying *paradigm change* and *ecological protection, forestry practices, First Nations' rights,* and *economic development.* The original statement (which, as I described in the previous chapter, was derived from multiple material and discursive practices) was passed along but changed form as more "hands" touched it. The broader emphasis that it gained – which I explore more fully in the next chapter – was already seen in the Coastal Rainforest Network's list of overarching goals (Econews 1996):

- protecting critical ecological areas;
- stopping all clearcutting in coastal temperate rainforests;
- limiting road construction in pristine areas;
- supporting First Nations' struggles to protect traditional territories; and
- promoting sustainable community economic development.

This list of goals was not uncontested, and internal disagreements eventually led to the demise of the Coastal Rainforest Network. However, while it held together, the alliance worked hard to make these goals a reality.

Representing the Rainforest

Obviously, the Coastal Rainforest Network was not initially in a position in which it could dictate land-use policy for the province; a list of goals was not enough. According to one environmentalist, "you need to generate power ... If you don't have power, you will just be considered some side input, and they will, you know, monkey-wrench around the edges to shift, to try to appease you, but if you don't have power you can't fundamentally alter the system."

How did ENGOs generate power in order to "fundamentally alter the system"? According to writers such as Hayter (2000, 2003), Marchak (1983), and Wilson (1998), control over British Columbia's forests was centralized through economic and political structures in the hands of a "development coalition" or "government-forest industry compact" (Wilson 1998, 81). In their analyses, this power can only be countered by an equal or greater power, such as the "powerful imperatives [of] neoliberalism, aboriginalism, and environmentalism" (Hayter 2003, 707). Similarly, in Wilson's (1998, 81) terms, industry's economic power can only be countered if environmentalists are able to "mobilize sufficient political resources to neutralize these advantages and push their issues onto the agenda." In other words, only the power of social structures can combat the power of social structures.

If the power of the forestry industry is explained simply as the product of economic forces such as capitalism, then the best that environmentalists can do is hope that other existing gigantic forces – such as science or social movements – can be invoked in opposition. However, as Latour (2005b, 252) argues, "if there is no way to inspect and decompose the contents of social forces, if they remain unexplained or overpowering, then there is not much that can be done." If one chooses to isolate one of the features of the network and then abstract it as the power of the market, of science, of economic resources, or of images, then one will have not only an impoverished explanation but also a tautological one. In contrast, a more pragmatic approach to power is to recognize that "only a skein of weak ties, of constructed, artificial, assignable, and surprising connections is the only way to begin contemplating any kind of fight" (Latour 2005b, 252). Or, in the words of John Law (1992, 2),

> if we want to understand the mechanics of power and organization it is important not to start out assuming whatever we wish to explain. For instance, it is a good idea not to take it for granted that there is a macrosocial system on the one hand, and bits and pieces of derivative microsocial detail on the other.

In contrast to the idea that power is centred and total, one can view power as a product of networks. In the case of the environmentalists' campaign, this took the form of their ability to use their status as representative of one network (the environment) to attack and intervene in another (the commodity chain). As one environmentalist interviewee noted, the "thing that the companies had to grapple with was that, you know, you needed to understand who had power and why they had it. And you needed to understand, look it, the environmental groups have power. Why do they have it? Well, they have it because they represent the environment." But what does it mean to "represent the environment"? Do environmentalists speak for the environment because it cannot speak for itself? Who has the authority to speak on behalf of the environment? In the GBR, environmentalists did not simply start speaking on behalf of the environment; they worked to designate a spokesperson for the rainforest – the grizzly bear – with which they could *share* speech (Latour 2005b, 64). That is, they enrolled the science of conservation biology to create an intermediary position between environmentalists who spoke on behalf of the environment and the environment speaking on its own behalf.

In the mid-1990s, W.D. Newmark (1995) published a study that demonstrated species loss from every national park in western North America. This study, along with the Sierra Club's map, prompted some people in the environmental community to reassess their strategies. One environmentalist noted that "a number of us in the environmental community sat back and said, 'okay, well, we're failing. Creating parks is not actually winning, it's failing.'" The Big Green Blob, in contrast, allowed environmentalists to see an entirely new kind of conservation opportunity for British Columbia, one built on the science of conservation biology. As one environmentalist mentioned, "we had an opportunity to do it right here – it's this huge landscape level, we can take a whole landscape conservation biology approach, it's not like we're just trying to protect the remnants that are left, like in southern BC, we could do it right from the beginning."

Environmentalists saw in conservation biology a form of expertise and authority that could oppose the political processes of land-use planning. In particular, they used conservation biology as a resource with which to oppose the official Land and Resource Management Plan (LRMP) process run by the provincial government (British Columbia 1996). ENGOs were very skeptical of the LRMP process and actively boycotted it. In particular, they were upset that the process did not conform to a conservation biology approach, with the result that "protected areas are in danger of becoming random exercises driven by political opportunity rather than biological necessity" (Canadian Rainforest Network 1998, 10). One environmentalist interviewed explained:

> We said, "well, we're not coming to the LRMP because it's basically set
> up to have a cookie-cutter outcome." It's the language we used, but
> the outcome is limited in its scope, and it's predetermined, and, in
> spite of the fact the government says that you can do whatever, there's a
> percentage of enhanced areas and a percentage of special management
> zones, a percentage of protected areas which they are working towards.

In 1997, the Coastal Rainforest Network commissioned a group of conservation biologists working for the Round River organization to develop a conservation area design (CAD) for the central coast. This project translated the coastal temperate rainforest and the great bear into terms associated with the "western science" of conservation biology (Jeo, Sanjayan, and Sizemore 1999, 12). Noting that the central and north coasts of British Columbia "represent some of the last remaining examples of intact coastal temperate rainforest – a globally rare ecosystem occupying less than 1% of the earth's land surface – [the authors] attempt[ed] to identify a system of conservation areas designed to protect and restore ecological values" (17). This project was intended to "ensure that future protected areas are designated based on conservation science rather than primarily on aesthetic, social, political, or economic considerations" (19). That is not to say, the authors quickly assured us, that "economic considerations are inconsequential. Rather, we believe that in order to maintain the application of the best available science to the CAD [conservation area design], socio-economic considerations can be brought to bear in a separate process after a biologically based CAD is complete" (19).

This focus perpetuates what Latour (1993) refers to as the modern constitution – that is, the tendency to simultaneously create new hybrids of humans and non-humans and purify these heterogeneous networks into the two collectors of society and nature. On the one hand, the authors mixed concepts from conservation biology and data about the coastal forests to designate a new representative for plants, animals, and ecological relationships. They thereby helped to fashion a new hybrid: the grizzly bear as a conservation design tool. This tool would then go on to intervene in networks linking trees, forestry companies, transportation systems, retail customers of forestry products, and consumers. On the other hand, the authors explicitly attempted to purify questions of ecology from "aesthetic, social, political, or economic considerations." As I note later, the problematic nature of this purification was eventually noticed and dealt with by some environmentalists, forming a key moment in the development of a good, common world for trees, animals, and people.

However, in the conservation area design, the authors argued that conservation decisions must be based solely on the interests of non-humans; only once their voices have been heard can other socio-economic interests be given a hearing. But how are the interests of non-humans to be taken into account? How can they be given voice if they cannot speak? It is important to note that the question of granting speech to non-humans is similar to the question of granting speech to humans (Callon 1986). Even if non-humans could articulate their interests in human speech, there are too many of them to be heard all at once, as is the case with people. As the authors noted, "many hundreds or thousands of species of yet unknown bacteria, fungi, invertebrates, plants, and even a few vertebrates, reside in BC's temperate rainforest, particularly in the soil or forest canopy. There is little hope for a comprehensive examination of all these species any time soon" (Jeo et al. 1999, 22). As such, these many beings and their interests need some form of representation. To deal with the impossibility of canvassing the needs of each species, conservation biologists have developed filtering techniques through which the multiple non-human interests of the rainforest can be captured. These filtering approaches are different from procedures in which people cast a ballot for a political representative, but they result in a spokesperson nonetheless (cf. Callon 1986, 13). One filtering technique, referred to as a *fine filter,* focuses on individual species as representatives of wider ecosystem functions and processes: "Because it is practically impossible (and possibly counter productive) to determine the ecological needs for every species resident in a region, researchers have suggested that instead of single species conservation plans, a suite of multiple focal species should be identified" (Jeo et al. 1999, 23).

As Jeo and colleagues (1999, 23) note, *focal species* are representatives of other species and ecological processes: "Focal species are selected such that their protection, as a group, would concurrently protect all or at least most remaining native species." One such focal species is the *umbrella species:* because of its large habitat and mobility requirement, "protection of umbrella species, by definition, provides protection of other native species" (24). In the conservation area design, grizzly bears are made to speak for the ecological interests of the coastal temperate rainforest. For one, grizzlies are chosen as a focal species to represent large carnivores, which "play a crucial and non-substitutable regulatory role in natural ecosystems" (29). For another, grizzlies are identified as "a classic umbrella species, that is, protection of grizzly bears would also protect a number of other species with similar habitat requirements and associations" (29).

Key grizzly habitat, the report argues, lies in the same areas targeted by the forestry industry – low-elevation, old-growth valley bottoms. Moreover, valley bottoms are the sites of salmon-bearing rivers. Salmon are identified in the conservation area design as a keystone species supporting numerous other species, including, importantly, grizzly bears. The habitat needs of salmon are identified as dependent on old growth and entire watersheds (Jeo et al. 1999, 48). In turn, old-growth forests – as a coarse filter – are identified as essential elements of a conservation design. In combination, grizzly habitat, salmon habitat, and old-growth forest overlap to produce the conservation area design's "*Core Conservation Areas* that comprise about 51% of the study area and include 74% of remaining old-growth forests and 61% of known salmon stocks" (56).

This filtering technique is designed to ensure that ecosystems and the biodiversity that they contain are adequately represented. To represent means, in a sense, that the representative speaks for the represented. But who is speaking for whom in conservation biology? Surely, it is the scientists who speak, since animals do not speak. However, scientists routinely design experiments and techniques to allow the "facts to speak for themselves." That is, they create devices and techniques that produce a *speech prosthesis* (Latour 2004) enabling these non-humans to become relevant to what is said about them and thus enabling their participation in the speech of humans. In the present case, non-humans are made to speak for other non-humans. The representatives selected through the science of conservation biology are hybrids: they are formed out of non-humans such as trees and animals, conceptual categories such as *ecosystem* and *focal species,* machines such as satellites and their photos, information such as vegetation data, and biologists who are calling for biologically based conservation strategies. It is this hybrid that is designated as a spokesperson for hundreds or thousands of species.

Does this spokesperson faithfully represent the others? According to Latour, representation is not an issue of correspondence, an either/or situation in which the representative either transparently represents the represented, thus achieving the status of truth, or fails to do so, thus presenting a falsehood. Rather, representation is a challenge, and speech is an impediment. As Latour (2004, 64) writes,

> with the notion of spokesperson, we are designating not the transparency of the speech in question, but the *entire gamut* running from complete doubt (I may be a spokesperson, but I am speaking in my own name and not in the name of those I represent) to total confidence (when I speak, it is really those I represent who speak through my mouth).

MOBILIZING SPOKESPERSONS FOR THE RAINFOREST

The generation of power involves more than representation – it also involves intervention in established networks of relationships. This often entails conflict. Conflict was a key aspect of environmentalists' quest to influence land-use decisions. As one environmentalist interviewee related, "the government employees all said yeah, if there wasn't a conflict – and the conflict is what led to us having power – then they wouldn't have heard us." On the one hand, building power involved a process of representing the interests of thousands of species and ecological processes of the environment in a single spokesperson. On the other, it involved processes of exposing and attacking the network constituting a seemingly single actor, the forestry industry. As one environmentalist noted, "we have to get power from somewhere, and so the market campaigns can target the companies, we can get the companies to agree to stop logging."

With much of the central and north coasts loaded into it, the great bear (and its relationship to salmon and old-growth trees) became a key actor mobilized to intervene in existing networks. In Callon's (1986, 14) terms, mobilization is a process of displacement and reassembly tied to representation by spokespeople. The plants and animals of the coastal forests are multiple, dispersed, and not easily accessible. But, through the filtering technique described above, they are displaced and rendered equivalent through the representative of the grizzly bear as an umbrella species. All of these beings are now capable of being transported along with the bear as their representative.

Some mobilizations of the grizzly bear were designed to develop interest in and support for the GBR. For example, in one publicity event in early April 1997, more than sixty activists dressed as grizzly, black, and "spirit" bears staged a demonstration at the corporate headquarters of International Forest Products, Western Forest Products, and MacMillan Bloedel. According to a Greenpeace (1997c) press release, "today the bears delivered eviction notices to the logging companies asking them to leave the rainforest, and carried signs that read, 'Clearcutting kills rainforest bears,' while sounds of chainsaws and bear growls accompanied the march." In another intervention in 1999, coastal grizzly bears travelled even farther, now taking the form of "Bella the grizzly bear." Bella travelled around the northeastern United States and Canada in a Sierra Club rainforest education bus to meet shareholders, students, interested members of the public, and environmentalists. The full-sized school bus was transformed into a "live rainforest interior," including moss, sounds of birds and streams, smells, replicas of small forest animals, and "Bella the grizzly bear fishing in a salmon stream" (Derworiz 1999).

These interventions were accompanied by claims about impending threats to the forests that the grizzly represented. For example, on April

21, 1997, Greenpeace released a report in Victoria, Toronto, five European cities (Amsterdam, Hamburg, London, Vienna, Zurich), and the United Nations and on the Internet. The report, entitled *Broken Promises: The Truth about What's Happening to British Columbia's Forests* (Greenpeace and Sierra Legal Defense Fund 1997), critically reviewed the New Democratic Party government's forestry policies, particularly the claim of "world-class forest practices," using government and industry data and on-site inspections. Among other things, the report argued that – despite claims to the contrary – clearcutting was still the dominant forest practice, that clearcuts exceeded size restrictions, that forests were cut right to stream banks, that clearcuts took place on steep, unstable slopes, and that clearcutting took place in special management zones designated for the protection of wildlife. These practices were all represented as direct threats to the great bear. Premier Clark responded by calling Greenpeace members "extremists who are trying to raise money and destroy British Columbia ... They are really enemies of British Columbia" (Hunter 1997). According to one company representative interviewee, this counterattack only strengthened environmentalists' resolve to work outside the official process.

The Impossible Locus of Local Blockades

In May 1997, environmental activists from Canada, Europe, and the United States flowed into the central and north coasts to engage in direct protests against logging companies. The first blockade was of the Western Forest Products operations on Roderick Island. Greenpeace sailed its ship *MV Moby Dick* up the coast to Green Inlet, close to Roderick Island, where members constructed a "mobile floating base camp" (McLintock 1997) that would house up to eight people (Curtis 1997b). Thirty activists from eight countries were aboard the vessel (Curtis 1997b). On May 21, 1997, eight activists from Austria, Germany, and Canada chained themselves to logging equipment on Roderick Island, hanging a banner that read "Stop Clearcutting the Great Bear Rainforest" beside a giant poster of a grizzly bear. At the same time, Greenpeace activists protested outside the Canadian Embassy in Bern, Switzerland (where they "returned" pulp originating from the central and north coasts); in Vienna, Austria, where a twenty-four-hour vigil took place in front of the Canadian Embassy; and in demonstrations in Seattle, Boston, and Washington, DC.

A representative of Western Forest Products described the multiple flows associated with the blockade:

> Greenpeace's ship arrived with their own helicopter – a used, $500 million helicopter – a ship, seventy-seven people, six satellite phones, and sixty people blockading the operations. I learned a lot about the environmental movement: they have far more resources than even a company that had a billion dollars worth of sales. We spent nine days ... on the front lines of me going out every morning to get the court injunction, to ask support, and the people locked to our equipment, whether they would be prepared to leave today. All videoed by ourselves, the BBC was there filming, plus Greenpeace had still photographers, and every single day they hired a turbo *Beaver* [sea plane], I hired a turbo *Beaver,* and the video was flown back to Vancouver, spliced for the seventeen stations down here.

Despite the multiple groups, locations, and technical mediations, environmental activists maintained an exclusive focus on biological values, failing to mention, for example, the area's local inhabitants – the Kitasoo First Nation. Not surprisingly, the Kitasoo people met protests on Roderick Island with resistance. Percy Starr of the Kitasoo First Nation asked the Greenpeace activists to leave, saying that the Kitasoo "are not happy with their [Greenpeace's] presence here. We realize we have problems, I mean everybody has them. But please give us the opportunity to try to resolve them ourselves" (cited in CBC 1997). Four days later a meeting of representatives of Western Forest Products, Greenpeace, and the Kitasoo took place. At the meeting, Chief Archie Robinson complained that Greenpeace was not acting with the consent of the Kitasoo: "This is our traditional territory. You did not ask us and we do not support civil disobedience. We are finding solutions and we will phone you when we need help" (cited in Curtis 1997c). The Kitasoo argued that they were involved in other activities to protect their land but that they were also focused on the real and pressing need for economic development.

To some extent, environmentalists' failure to consider the interests of First Nations was rectified at a second blockade – this time of Interfor's operations on King Island. In June 1997, the Nuxalk House of Smayusta (an elders' council) extended an invitation to environmentalists to join their protest.[1] Greenpeace, Forest Action Network, Bearwatch, and PATH (People's Action for Threatened Habitat) joined protesters on King Island (where they hung a banner reading "Protect the Great Bear Rainforest").

On June 6, 1997, fifty-five members of the Nuxalk First Nation and environmentalists blockaded Interfor's access to its tree licence, shutting down its operations for nineteen days. Twenty-four people, including six Nuxalk, were arrested.

However, while local First Nations organized this blockade, the presence of environmentalists was not supported by all Nuxalk and certainly not by the elected chiefs:

> Nuxulk [sic] elected Chief Archie Pootlass said Monday the protesters are "environmental colonialists." "They're not listening to the Nuxulk people. We had a meeting about this on Friday and the clear majority of the Nuxulk people don't support this protest. Most of the Nuxulk people feel they can solve their own problems without Greenpeace coming in and telling the local people what's best for them," he said. "They're splitting families and driving a wedge in," he said. "It's really sad to see the Nuxulk people divided." (Hall 1997)

The protests on Roderick Island and King Island were local, direct actions in the coastal forests themselves. Yet, at the same time, the protests involved many extra-local elements. Were these protests local or global? According to Latour (2005b, 194), the "local" is an implausible locus; instead, "what has been designated by the term 'local interaction' is the assemblage of all the other local interactions distributed elsewhere in time and space, which have been brought to bear on the scene through the relays of various non-human actors." Decisions to launch direct, local protests against Western Forest Products and Interfor were made in Greenpeace's Ancient Forest Campaign headquarters in Vancouver. The ability to make these decisions, in turn, was supported by fundraisers on the streets of cities in Canada, Europe, and the United States. Funders, fundraisers, and campaign strategists were able to act at a distance (Latour 1987) by deploying the *MV Moby Dick* and its impressive "resources" to particular sites in the GBR. That these sites are implausible as loci of (solely) face-to-face interactions is given by the fact that "there are a great number of agencies swarming toward them" (Latour 2005b, 196), some of which come from different places, some of which come from different times, some of which apply greater degrees of influence than others, and some of which are non-human.

The connections established among the coastal forests and publics, the media, and environmentalists in Canada, Europe, and the United States did not erase the locality of the GBR by placing it in a global context but performed a local area of international concern and local, direct protest by progressively connecting it to a wider network of actors. Circulations of the rainforest in a travelling bus, bear costumes worn by activists, environmentalists on a floating base camp, and conflict filmed, flown, and uplinked to satellite – these flows connected the central coast to other agencies. In this sense, the issue expanded not from the local to the global but in terms of the size of the network.

Nevertheless, as the GBR became more connected and better articulated, it took on the aspect of a global issue. For one, following the hard work of scientists and activists, ENGOs were able to circulate a total panorama of the GBR. For another (following the flow in the opposite direction from that which produced local, direct protest), the issue expanded out to other agencies in other countries. It was not as if the region did not have any outside connections before environmentalists' network-building activities. The provincial government based in Victoria, logging companies based in Vancouver, and loggers based in northern Vancouver Island all flowed into and out of the region, through legislation and regulations, tenure, and machinery and workers flown into and out of logging camps. In addition, the logging companies were connected to the customers of their products, most of whom were located in the United States, Europe, and Japan. It was precisely the latter flows that environmentalists exploited to expand their issue. As explained by one environmentalist,

> we can't win this by blockading. That's been the strategy of the environmental movement: blockade and media. One, you can't get people up there, either the media or the blockaders – you couldn't sustain it. So that's actually not even a viable tactic for us. So we need to do something different, and the markets work has started in Clayoquot, so the markets work was, you know, refocused on the Great Bear as the power or the leverage.

Just as we can locate the local via its connections to other agencies swarming toward it, so too we can ask who, what, and where the global market is. In particular, we can inquire into how the marketplace is connected to the local sites of logging operations in the coastal forests. As Latour (2005b, 183) explains,

> whenever anyone speaks of a "system," a "global feature," a "structure," a "society," an "empire," a "world economy," an "organization," the first ANT reflex should be to ask: "in which building? In which bureau? Through

which corridor is it accessible? Which colleagues has it been read to? How has it been compiled?"

In fact, we do not have to engage in this inquiry ourselves, since answering these questions is precisely the task that ENGOs set for themselves.

THE MARKET CAMPAIGN

The Coastal Rainforest Coalition launched the market campaign on June 10, 1997 (halfway through the King Island blockade), sending letters to 5,000 companies urging them to phase out wood and paper products that derive from British Columbia's old-growth coastal forests (Curtis 1997a). Given the large number of companies targeted, however, environmentalists likely did not know for certain whether all the companies in fact purchased products originally deriving from British Columbia's coastal forests. More targeted approaches ensued after this initial mailing, modelled after strategies developed in the campaign for Clayoquot Sound:

> [During the Clayoquot Sound conflict,] we started tracing the products. At the time with very little resources we were literally following trucks, pretending to be students and going on mill tours. Where is it going? Who's buying it? And so what we found is that the far majority of what's happening in Canada, the logging in Canada, is going to the United States. (Berman 2006a)

Environmental groups drew on this experience to trace the linkages between forestry companies with operations and rights in the central and north coasts and their customers. The market campaigns were primarily conducted by the Coastal Rainforest Coalition (formerly the Clayoquot Rainforest Coalition and soon to become ForestEthics), Forest Action Network, Greenpeace, Rainforest Action Network, Natural Resources Defense Council, and the Sierra Club. In the first step, as one environmentalist interviewee noted, forest products were traced to buyers:

> We did a whole variety of things: from electronically tracking sales to people walking around lumberyards and looking at the wrapping on wood in Home Depot or in wherever. And through that you could figure it out ... And so as the boats [arrived] in Amsterdam, you could ... watch what was loaded and unloaded. So it was some pretty grassroots

techniques ... The other thing was a product called red cedar [that] could easily be tracked because red cedar only comes from a very limited part of the world, so if you are selling red cedar, likely it's coming from British Columbia.

Using these techniques, environmentalists identified traces of networks. To the average person walking past a construction site, a pile of lumber would look like little more than a pile of lumber. To activists aware of the commodity chain, however, the label identifying Western Forest Products was enough for them to see a network linking the lumber back to British Columbia's coastal forests. Such strategies enabled environmentalists to more or less map out the entire commodity chain, as shown in the figure on the opposite page. In this schematic, a consumer blithely goes about shopping, seemingly unaware of the many chains connecting him or her to a network of other agencies. However, any product that ends up in the shopping cart while he or she strolls around Walmart, Home Depot, or Oakwood Homes – whether it is toothpaste, clothing, paper, furniture, or lumber – derives from the processing work of other big companies. Moreover, these companies had to get their raw materials from somewhere. If we continue to follow the schematic, we see chains connecting the companies to lumber and pulp mills. And where did these mills get their materials? From the logging companies, surrounded by seas of stumps. These companies, of course, are connected by a chain to the "ancient forests" of Canada. As a result of these chains, as one ENGO statement argues, "Canada's rainforests are being destroyed to provide the British public with magazines, garden furniture, DIY [do it yourself] products, ladders, household doors, conservatories, garden sheds, and even food products" (Fong and McCabe 1998).

Interestingly, just as with the conservation area design, one can discern both an "explicitation" of the networks connecting humans and non-humans and an attempt to sever such connections. On the one hand, forests are connected to consumers through myriad chains identified and traced by environmentalists themselves. On the other, these chains are severed since the schematic contains two major parts. The first part consists of the non-human world of ancient forests. The second part consists of a human world of production and consumption. The impression that one gets looking at such a schematic is that (1) consumers must be made aware of how the products they purchase are connected to BC's forests through several chains and (2) that they should cease making such purchases in order to sever the connection between industry and the forests.

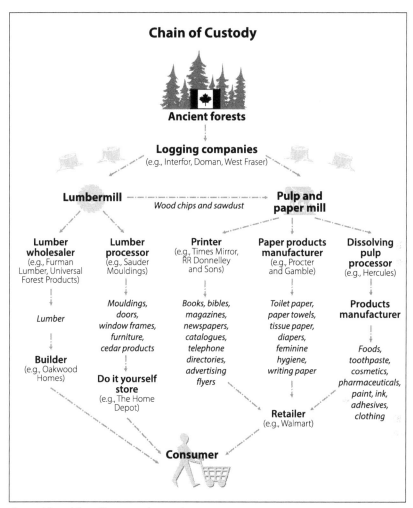

Chain of Custody

Ancient forests

Logging companies
(e.g., Interfor, Doman, West Fraser)

Lumbermill — Wood chips and sawdust — Pulp and paper mill

| Lumber wholesaler (e.g., Furman Lumber, Universal Forest Products) | Lumber processor (e.g., Sauder Mouldings) | Printer (e.g., Times Mirror, RR Donnelley and Sons) | Paper products manufacturer (e.g., Procter and Gamble) | Dissolving pulp processor (e.g., Hercules) |

Lumber

Mouldings, doors, window frames, furniture, cedar products

Books, bibles, magazines, newspapers, catalogues, telephone directories, advertising flyers

Toilet paper, paper towels, tissue paper, diapers, feminine hygiene, writing paper

Products manufacturer

Foods, toothpaste, cosmetics, pharmaceuticals, paint, ink, adhesives, clothing

Builder (e.g., Oakwood Homes)

Do it yourself store (e.g., The Home Depot)

Retailer (e.g., Walmart)

Consumer

Source: Adapted from Greenpeace (1999, 13).

Activists targeted the commodity chain at several points, moving from the sites of logging operations to the transportation of logs, to sites of manufacturing, to the transportation of products to retail customers, and finally – and most effectively – to the sites of sale of the final products. For example, on June 24, 1997, in British Columbia, Greenpeace activists boarded the log barge *The Seaspan Rigger.* The ship transported logs to processing facilities in British Columbia. According to the organization's press release, the ship was used to transport old-growth rainforest trees, such as red cedar and hemlock, "for minimal processing before export to

Asia, Europe, and the United States" (Greenpeace 1997a). Using what would become the main message of such protests, the activists attached a banner reading "Don't Buy Rainforest Destruction – Greenpeace."

Protesters also targeted the transportation of forest products after they had been processed into other products. On August 21, 1997, Greenpeace activists pointed out the origins of pulp and dimensional lumber en route to Europe and the United States aboard the ship *Saga Wind*. The forest products belonged to Doman Industries, the parent company of Western Forest Products. Protesters spray-painted the word *clearcut* with a slash through it on the side of the ship and attempted to hang a banner across the bow reading "This Ship Exports Rainforest Destruction" (Greenpeace 1997b) before being knocked off the ship with high-pressure hoses (Curtis 1997d). The action was justified by Greenpeace in terms of the need to draw attention to the commodity chain: "Right now, in the absence of a clear eco-labelling system, there's absolutely no way they could know that these products come [from the central coast of British Columbia]" (Greenpeace 1997b).

Activists also targeted the *Saga Wind* when it made port to unload its cargo. On March 27, 1998, Greenpeace activists boarded the ship as it docked in Scotland. The ship was carrying 3,000 tonnes of wood pulp and about 200,000 board feet of plywood for Western Forest Products. The activists scaled a crane and unfurled a banner that read "Don't Buy Canada's Great Bear Rainforest Destruction" (Pemberton 1998). Two months later the ship was targeted in the Belgian port of Antwerp, where Greenpeace activists spray-painted on the ship's hull "Don't buy rainforest destruction. Stop Doman and Interfor!" ("BC Logging Protests" 1998). In December, activists targeted the ship as it made port in the Netherlands. In May, activists boarded the freighter *Saga River* on the Weser River near Bremerhaven, Germany, that was carrying pulp from Western Forest Products, unfurling a banner reading "Don't Do Business with Rainforest Destructors" (Greenpeace 1998b).

Other shipments of forest products were also targeted. For example, on October 20, 1998, Greenpeace activists boarded the ship *Thorseggen* as it tried to make port in Long Beach, California. The ship was carrying newsprint made by a mill supplied with wood chips from Interfor. Activists chained themselves to the ship's unloading cranes and unfurled a banner reading "Stop Destroying the Great Bear Rainforest." According to the organization's press release, "Greenpeace has evidence that large quantities of wood chips from ancient coastal rainforests are being sent to the mills which provide this newsprint to California customers – including The Los

Angeles Times, GTE, ATandT, and the Orange County Register" (Greenpeace 1998a).

The primary purpose of these actions was to render explicit the chains connecting the coastal forests to cycles of production and consumption. Before this intervention, consumers did not know where products such as pulp and lumber came from. Industrial and retail customers (and their customers) encountered these products as simple things unconnected to other things. But environmentalists claimed that customers were "destroying the Great Bear Rainforest." How could they make this claim? Customers were not even in the same country as the forests, let alone wielding chainsaws and cutting them down. However, as environmentalists discovered, there are direct links connecting the products to British Columbia's coastal forests. Simply by rendering these networks explicit, ENGOs indicated that, when a company or an individual purchased a product, they were actually acting at a distance (Latour 1987, 219). Customers thought that they were simply buying products, but they were participating in rainforest destruction since the products that they purchased were linked through a commodity chain to the forests.

Actions are not performed by individuals but by networks, or, in Latour's (2005b, 45) terms, "action is overtaken." That is, customers' purchases are taken over and translated by other entities, resulting in particular outcomes in a forest far away. Customers' seemingly local and delimited purchases of forest products are connected via transportation technologies to manufacturers that in turn are connected to logging companies that in turn are connected to the forests. At each link along this chain, forests become translated – into logs, pulp, lumber, wood chips, paper, furniture, clothing, and so on. If the entire chain is maintained, then an action at one point will have effects at another point, with the result that ENGOs can claim that customers' actions have effects on distant forests.

Transforming Companies into Activists

From 1997 to 1999, environmental organizations put pressure on industrial and retail buyers of pulp, paper, and dimensional lumber, including companies that use pulp to create fabrics and glues, paper users, paper sellers, home builders, lumber sellers, furniture stores, and, perhaps most significantly, do-it-yourself home improvement stores. When ENGOs targeted these companies, they took on, in a sense, the "global capitalist market." However, while a company such as Home Depot is very big in the sense that it has big box stores, many stores in many countries, many employees, and large profits, it is not big in the sense of a capitalist social structure that dominates puny individuals (Latour 2005b, 178-79). Latour (2005b, 176) uses the term "oligopticon" to refer to powerful actors that give the impression of operating within a social structure through their many connections:

> As soon as the local sites that manufacture global structures are underlined [with the notion of the oligopticon], it is the entire topography of the social world that is being modified. Macro no longer describes a *wider* or a *larger* site in which the micro would be embedded ... but another equally local, equally micro place, which is *connected* to many others through some medium transporting specific types of traces ... What is now highlighted much more vividly than before are all the connections, the cables, the means of transportation, the vehicles linking places together. This is their strength but also ... their frailty.

As ENGOs found, companies such as Home Depot exist as networks that are only as strong as their weakest link, which, in its case, took the form of consumer preference. If ENGOs could stigmatize the companies' brands, then they could sever the companies from their customers – the consumers (Conroy 2007). In fact, it turned out that this link is so weak that all ENGOs had to do was raise the spectre of a boycott of companies that purchase products deriving from British Columbia's central and north coasts. Since Home Depot was the "largest retailer of wood products in the world" (Greenpeace 1999, 18), and since it sold products from British Columbia's coastal forests, including mouldings made by Sauder Mould-ings (a corporate affiliate of Interfor), the company became the target of a sustained campaign. Environmentalists met with Home Depot execu-tives, sent over 8,000 letters and postcards to Home Depot, and staged numerous demonstrations, including ten protests in the western US states in September 1998, seventy-five protests in the United States and Canada in October 1998, weekly protests during January and February 1999 at new Home Depot openings, and 150 demonstrations at Home Depot stores in the United States and Canada on March 17, 1999 (Stansbury 2000).

Just as with their actions on the freighters, environmentalists' goal was to "explicitate" (Latour 2007, 2) the networks connecting commodities for sale in Home Depot's stores to the forests from which they derived. While previously customers could walk into a store and pick up a 2×4 with the only considerations being quality and price, ENGOs showed that the products were not simply 2×4s (or other simple commodities) but connected to other places, beings, and issues. In other words, the purchase of a 2×4 became connected to a host of unintended consequences; as one banner put it, "Ancient Forest Destruction: On Sale Now at the Home Depot." Or, in the terms of an industry representative, "you can't sell a 2×4 with a protester hanging off of it." This network, of course, was represented by the great bear, now taking the form of a forty-foot inflatable bear that travelled to most protests in Europe and the United States.

Home Depot was just one target (if a key one) in a larger European, American, and Japanese campaign. On September 29, 1997, BandQ – Europe's largest do-it-yourself furniture maker – announced that it would cease to purchase BC hemlock and move to pine in an effort to avoid lumber harvested in unsustainable ways. Signalling the fact that the company had switched alliances from lumber companies to activist networks, this move was framed as a protest by news media: "In a protest against logging practices in British Columbia, one of Great Britain's largest do-it-yourself furniture makers has decided to boycott B.C. hemlock, the predominant species on the West Coast" (Matas 1997). Cancellations started to pick up in 1998 after Greenpeace UK officially launched its market campaign in March, at which time it already had secured cancellations by BandQ, Sainsbury's Homebase, and Do It All. The United Kingdom was the largest European importer of BC forest products.

Environmentalists led by the Coastal Rainforest Coalition (made up of Greenpeace, Rainforest Action Network, and Natural Resources Defense Council) also attacked forestry companies' largest customers in the United States. By April 1, 1998, Greenpeace (1998c) claimed US cancellations from "California-based HomeBase, Inc. (the third most profitable do-it-yourself chain in the country), Xerox, Kinkos, 3M, Bristol-Myers-Squibb, FedEx, and two Fortune 500 firms who wish not to be publicly identified at this time." It also added Magnet stores, BBC magazines, and German do-it-yourself stores to its European list. Combined cancellations totalled tens of millions of dollars of logging contracts, according to the organization.

Environmentalists soon claimed that twenty-seven major companies had joined them to become activists. An advertisement placed by environmental groups in the *New York Times* on December 8, 1998, states "how leading U.S. companies are saving ancient rainforests without ever chaining themselves to a tree." The ad displays a large photograph of a forested valley (taken by Ian McAllister), below which is a text box listing companies that are "leading the way in the protection of ancient forests." Further below, and adjacent to a photograph of a clear cut valley, is another text box that lists companies that are "lagging behind." This ad both renders networks explicit and seeks to purify them. On the one hand, it makes it clear that forests are connected to businesses and the decisions that they make. The connection is emphasized through placement of the text in relation to the photograph of the forests. The title sentence starts outside the picture frame but ends within it. This suggests that the companies can act at a distance with respect to the forests: they are outside the forests but can nevertheless reach into them, acting on them without physical contact (chaining themselves). This ability is explained in the accompanying text, which suggests that companies "have committed to survey their wood and paper suppliers, shift away from old growth to independently certified or alternative materials, and to reduce overall virgin wood fiber use." In other words, the companies seek to render explicit the networks connecting them to the forests in order to ensure that the products they purchase do not adversely impact the forests.

On the other hand, these connections were purified into business and nature since the overall goal of the campaign was to sever these companies from British Columbia's coastal forests. The text box containing the "leading US companies" is separated from the intact, unprotected river valley displayed above. Activism ("chaining themselves to a tree") is admitted within the frame, while business remains outside it. Thus, even though business is linked to activism and conservation, it remains outside "virgin" nature. The choice is presented in stark terms: there are those "leading" companies that have chosen to "save what cannot be replaced" and those that have not made such a choice and are thus destroying forests. Good companies, connected to the preservation of a separate nature, are contrasted with bad, "lagging" companies, connected to a destroyed landscape. The latter companies are placed in a separate box in the ad.

Interestingly, while there are stark differences between "lagging" companies and environmentalists, just as there are between the intact valley and the logged valley, the lines start to become more permeable between environmentalists and "leading" companies. As noted, the title sentence is both inside and outside pristine nature, previously the sole responsibility of environmentalists. Companies are now represented as environmental activists. Moreover, no line delimits the top of the box containing the companies that are "leading the way in the protection of ancient rainforests." The ad identifies a commonality between environmentalists and companies, between business and conservation, so much so that environmentalists are forced to distance themselves somewhat even while they tout the companies' good business decisions. As the ad states, "we don't always agree with these companies on other issues, but today we roundly applaud them for their leadership in helping to save the world's ancient forests." As this sentence indicates, there is some tension or ambiguity with respect to the relationship between environmentalists and businesses that are on their side of the issue. ENGOs simultaneously recognize connections and purify them, thus reproducing the modern constitution; however, in doing so, they create the possibility for a new approach not built on the premature equivalence of "ancient forests" with non-human nature.

A key moment in the campaign involved mobilizing retail customers themselves. In August 1999, ENGOs sponsored a tour of British Columbia's coastal forests for a German pulp and paper association and an association of German magazine publishers. The associations, which had previously toured the coastal forests with forest companies and the provincial government, were now given a tour by ENGOs. According to the forestry company representative allowed to accompany the tour but not to comment, the ENGOs turned the tour into a striking performance:

Interviewee: We flew into a cut block, and it was just an ordinary ... Forest Practices Code coastal cut block: it was about a twenty-hectare clearcut. And the Greenpeace Germany forest campaigner, Thomas Henningson, gathered everybody around – in quite a dramatic way – standing well into the cut block (and it was on the side of a hill, not real steep, but a gentle hill like that, and we were at the top end of it, and you could see all around), and he pulled out this silviculture prescription for this block, which he had obtained. And it said in the prescription, in the column where it lists the type of harvest system, it said, "clearcut with reserves." But this was a clearcut.

JP: There were no reserves?

Interviewee: ... No, here's the thing: it was actually a thirty-five-hectare block, and so there was like twelve or fourteen hectares in the reserve, but it was on the edge of the block. It was not in the middle or scattered or distributed, it was on the edge. So what you were looking at was a clearcut, right? This astounded the Germans; they felt like they had been lied to by both the province and by industry.

After the tour (which took four days and eighteen and a half hours of flying time on two helicopters), the associations requested a meeting with ENGOs, forestry companies, and the government. According to the facilitator of the meeting, it was one of those meetings that I will never forget. [Laughter]. Ah, they were, they were just – to suggest that they were furious would be an understatement. They felt that they had been lied to by the provincial government, deceived by the industry as well – they made those statements in the meeting. One of them, the chair of the group, or the fellow that was the de facto chair of the group, the delegation, was just shaking with rage at one point in the meeting. Holding up a picture of a cut block and pointing to it, and it had something to do with in-stand retention and how it had been calculated, [he] said, "you lied to us."

The two business associations, which together represented significant contracts for forestry companies, threatened to cancel the contracts if the land-use conflict could not be resolved. At the same meeting, word was received that Home Depot was changing its procurement policies and making a commitment to purchase Forest Stewardship Council certified forest products. These events, in addition to previous contract cancellations, shifted forest industries' networks in a significant manner, as one company representative indicated: "It was really there that I think was the turning point where they decided that they needed to take a different approach. You had some companies that were beginning to believe that they were sort of one protest away from losing significant contracts." In other words, the environmentalists' efforts were successful. They convinced activists that it was in their interest to help build a movement to protect the coastal temperate rainforest to the north, rather than to focus on isolated valleys to the south. In making the grizzly bear the "spokesperson" for the rainforest, environmentalists also managed to shift authority away from the provincial government and its "cookie-cutter" land-use planning process to a process driven more by the interests and requirements of animals, trees, and ecological systems. Then, after "explicitating" the network linking coastal forests to products for sale around the world, environmentalists used the same network to their advantage, using it to sever forestry companies from their retail customers. Once retail customers began to shift their identities, interests, and allegiances to environmental concerns, the forestry companies were forced to follow suit. In response, BC forestry companies came together to discuss how they might collectively address ENGOs' demands. This was a significant development that induced a shift in environmentalists' approach to wilderness politics from limits associated with the modern constitution to attempts to craft one good common collective for humans and non-humans alike.

3

Negotiating with the Enemy

Articulating a Common Matter of Concern

The process of network formation is not simple. It involves a great deal of work, resources, time, and movement. Moreover, this work is not a one-way process: network elements often contest the terms of their inclusion and place conditions on their participation. Network enrolment, therefore, is a process of negotiation that might be more or less difficult. For example, the wilderness preservation movement initially resisted the tactics of personal growth and spirituality at the activist retreat but eventually came together to form the Canadian Rainforest Network in order to campaign for protection of the GBR. Grizzly bears, for their part, demonstrated little resistance to their enrolment as representatives of the forests through conservation biology, education, and activism. Other groups were more recalcitrant. While ENGOs successfully severed forestry companies from their customers, forestry companies fought ENGOs every step of the way. They were traditional enemies, and it would take a great deal of negotiation and concession to get forestry companies on board. Similarly, First Nations rejected the roles ascribed to them by ENGOs. They might have had a degree of overlap in their interests in the land with environmentalists – particularly with respect to conservation – but these interests derived from very different sources.

Enrolment often provokes resistance because it involves the translation of identities and interests. However, it is important to recognize that the enroller as well as the enrolled undergo processes of translation. ENGOs initiated the process of network formation and positioned themselves as an *obligatory point of passage (OPP)* (Callon 1986) for other groups. The

OPP forms the centre of network formation, the point through which actors must pass in order to realize their interests. The OPP simultaneously hinders and facilitates realization of groups' interests since it puts itself in their way and suggests that groups can realize their interests only by going through it. For example, retail customers of BC forest products could now attain sales only if they joined activists in boycotting BC forestry companies. However, once groups join a network, its centre begins to shift and change as the new elements demand a reciprocal translation in the identities and interests of the network's convener. If ENGOs were to realize the vision for which they had assembled a network of support, they would have to let go of it. They would be forced to shift their identities and interests as they became connected to forestry companies and First Nations. Moreover, ENGOs' attempts to solidify the matter of concern into pristine wilderness in need of protection would face resistance. As Latour (2004, 244) explains, *matters of concern* are open ended rather than indisputable, fabricated rather than discovered, produced by multiple groups rather than by experts alone, and explicitly recognize potential unintended consequences.

Engaging the Forestry Industry with Love

ENGOs were not unchallenged during their European and American campaigns. The forestry industry and the BC government flew delegations to Europe to refute claims being made about BC forest practices. Wherever the delegations went, the ENGOs followed, protesting and handing out information. On the other hand, the provincial government tagged along with ENGOs. As one activist interviewee noted,

> I did a freedom of information request – actually David Boyd did it when he was working with UVic Law – and he somehow got this binder – it's about this thick [shows with hands] – that was all of the consulates and embassy people and CSIS that were actually privately or secretly following me around from presentation to presentation and doing full critiques of my talks.

Nevertheless, the forestry companies came to realize that they were unlikely to counter ENGOs' campaigns through this trade mission approach. As noted by an industry representative, "people had been out there spending a lot of money, a lot of resources, talking to customers, making trips to

Europe, bringing customers over, going down to the United States, doing the regular, kind of, 'PR' stuff, and it was clear that it wasn't, you know, that it wasn't working."

In response, the chief operating officer of MacMillan Bloedel convened a series of weekly meetings for coastal BC forestry companies in April 1999 (Stansbury 2000). The purpose of the informal meetings was to develop a common approach among affected forestry companies to deal with the ENGOs' market campaign. In June 1999, a caucus was formed out of Western Forest Products, Interfor, Weyerhaeuser (formerly MacMillan Bloedel), Canfor, Norske Canada (now Catalyst Paper), and West Fraser "to develop and manage [a] more coordinated industry strategy moving forward" (Coady and Smith 2003, 6). After Home Depot's announcement of its new procurement policy and the German associations' demands, this idea was given impetus, and in January 2000 the industry caucus created the Coast Forest Conservation Initiative (CFCI).

The forestry companies created this initiative because of environmentalists' *interessement* between them and their customers. Since ENGOs had successfully enrolled retail customers through their "explicitation" of the commodity chain and the spectre of consumer boycott, forestry companies had to transform themselves into suitable environmental identities if they were to retain customers. The companies thereby self-enrolled in environmentalists' networks, translating themselves to say, in effect, "we're environmentalists too." As noted by one company representative, "CFCI's strategy from day one has been – not from day one but early on – has been to capture the stage, the high ground, so that they could say they were more, or as, ecosystem conscious and EBM conscious as any environmentalist."

The initiative also involved the formation of a space to negotiate with the ENGOs. According to one of the participants, "we formed a caucus of the companies to see if we could work as a caucus. And we wrote up an internal paper for the companies about a kind of a standstill." This "standstill" period would be defined by an agreement in which companies would defer logging if ENGOs would agree to suspend their market campaign. In this conflict-free zone, companies and ENGOs would negotiate a permanent agreement.[1]

Negotiations began as acrimoniously as could have been expected given a history of conflict stretching back to the fight over South Moresby Island on Haida Gwaii (Queen Charlotte Islands) and Clayoquot Sound – not to mention more recent conflicts over the central and north coasts – that was not easily overcome. The relationship between ENGOs and forestry companies, after all, had been institutionalized as war – the war in the woods. One of the main negotiators for the ENGOs described negotiations as a violent conflict:

> [Industry said,] "okay, we'll sit down and try to figure things out,"
> but, at that point in '99, we would sit down and have conversations,
> and I used to describe it as, you know, we would go in there with
> our Plexiglas riot gear in front of us and put it down and shoot bullets
> across the table. And, you know, they would have their Plexiglas up, and
> all the bullets would fall down, and then we would put up ours, and they
> would put theirs down and shoot at us, and all the bullets would fall on
> the table. That's what our conversations were like, nobody was listening
> to each other. It was so hostile, and people hated each other. Like, they
> didn't even know each other to hate each other, we hated each other's
> positions, we hated each other's sectors, and it was deep, you know,
> Haida Gwaii, Clayoquot Sound, it was all kind of built up to this
> where both parties just detested each other.

The opposition between ecology and economy was nowhere as pronounced as in that room. At one point early in the negotiations, the facilitator simply left the room, letting the parties yell at each other with no expectation that anything constructive would come of it. Two "sectors" or "positions" squared off against one another, each trying to destroy the other. Each was a caricature for the other: for environmentalists, forestry companies wanted to wilfully destroy ecosystems in order to enrich themselves; for forestry companies, environmentalists wanted to put people out of work to feel good about themselves. They "hated" each other: there was a clear boundary between their positions, as clear and solid as a Plexiglas shield. None of what environmentalists wanted was in forestry companies and vice versa. They were as different from each other as two groups could be. Despite (or even because of) the networks linking ecology and economy that environmentalists had traced, their goal was to enforce a strict boundary between the forests and the forestry companies. This boundary became blurred, however, with an interesting shift in environmentalists' strategy, as one interviewee noted:

> We started doing this thing called a "love strategy" where we would walk
> into rooms with people who we traditionally had called enemies – like
> the forest industry who were cutting down our friends, the trees – and

we would walk in, and we would try to find the one thing in them that we could love and nurture and support and help that part of them make the right decision.

While environmentalists originally perceived forestry company CEOs as representatives of sectors with singular positions inimical to their own, they came to see them as complex people. Rather than standing in as a synecdoche for the evil forestry industry, the individuals with whom environmentalists negotiated came to be seen as human beings with potential qualities that one could connect to and thus nurture (something discovered in the Clayoquot campaigns; see Berman 2011). This change in approach sought not only to bring useful qualities out of forestry company officials but also to honour and validate those qualities, thus exercising the "compassion" instilled in the Hollyhock training sessions, as one environmentalist interviewee noted:

We used to come up the elevator and go, "okay, so we've got to love them, we have to love them, we have to love them ..." We'd go up the elevator, and we'd do that, a lot of it came from here [referring to Hollyhock], right? Crazy, flaky, weirdo shit – whatever – but it's really a piece of the story, it really defines what happened, coming out the other end.

According to this participant, the impact of this shift was originally unintended:

The interesting thing is, so we're now in this love strategy piece, and we're all about bringing the best of people to the table and trying, ourselves, to model it but also creating space for other people, and they don't know that's what we're doing, they're just having the experience of whatever it is that we are doing. And they're all kind of freaked out because they don't know what to make of us because we're so young and we don't negotiate the way they have all been trained to negotiate, and nothing is making sense whatsoever, basically. And they're just constantly sort of, slightly, "what are they coming up with next?" kind of thing. And for two years, I think we made huge gains just by virtue of the fact that they were just off balance, they just couldn't figure out where we were coming from, and they didn't understand this whole love thing.

Love involves a form of empathy that, in turn, entails a degree of commonality or sharing. When these environmentalists practised the "love strategy," they began to identify and empathize with forestry company representatives. They therefore put down their Plexiglas shields to breach the boundary between them. This must indeed have been a confusing experience for forestry companies. However, this participant mentioned, eventually the forestry company representatives "kind of got it. And not that they got it at some language level, or that there was words around it or anything, but they all of a sudden got that we weren't interested in being enemies anymore, but what we were interested in doing was finding solutions together." The basic strategy was to listen, to acknowledge the obstacles facing the forestry industry, to try to craft a framework that would solve them: "The love strategy was more, exactly that, let's go sit down and listen to them. Find out what their problems are and how we can solve them." With the boundary between them blurred, forestry companies' problems became environmentalists' problems – a prerequisite for "finding solutions together."

EXCHANGING PROPERTIES IN A NEW SOLUTION SPACE

Out of these negotiations, the two sides produced a "standstill agreement"[2] specified in a Letter of Intent (Joint Solutions Project 2000),[3] which simultaneously specified the new relationship between ENGOs and forestry companies and positioned them as a new obligatory point of passage for groups with an interest in BC coastal forests. The first task was to create space in which these new relationships could be established. According to the Letter of Intent, the purpose of the agreement was to "establish a conflict free period within which the parties can work collaboratively on developing recommendations with the provincial government, First Nations, and stakeholders on a conservation-biology/ecosystem-based plan for the north and central coast, including recommendations on protected areas" (Joint Solutions Project 2000, 4). Why did the parties think that they needed to create a "space" or forum in which to discuss land-use options for coastal British Columbia? Wasn't there already a forum tasked with precisely that purpose – the multi-stakeholder Central Coast Land Resource Management Plan (CCLRMP)? The problem with that forum, as described in Chapter 2, was its "cookie-cutter" approach to land-use planning. While it was a public forum that considered multiple interests, the LRMP was unable to create the kind of space needed to come up with truly innovative solutions. Instead, the LRMP actually reinforced opposition rather than facilitated compromise. For example, an environmentalist interviewee suggested,

> in the big public arena, they're [the union] not going to admit that they've got to change anyways, but we could sit down and have a meeting with the IWA [Industrial Wood and Allied Workers of Canada] and say, "look, the writing is on the wall, like there aren't any trees left for you on Vancouver Island. Your industry has to change, your union has to change, right?" They knew that, but they would never, the way the LRMP was set up, it was set up, in spite of what I think people wanted, it was just set up where people took positions, because in a public space like that, with the government recording it, they're not going to admit to certain things. You need to create a space where people can admit to that or maybe not even admit to it but find a solution around it.

In British Columbia, the modern constitution played out in a "big public arena": the agora. This is where politics was performed, but it was unwieldy because of the way in which it turned groups into inflexible positions. This is where the war in the woods and its "trees versus jobs" dynamic played out. With the government recording these positions and judging winners and losers (within a balance or trade-off framework), divisions became stark. How could the divisions be softened? How could common solutions be forged? A new "space" outside the agora needed to be crafted. The first task was to remove the scorekeeper, the provincial government, as one environmentalist indicated:

> We're sitting down *without* the provincial government, who, generally speaking, are an anchor in all these processes, they just drag on you and stop you from doing innovative things. They are very risk averse. So we got them out of the room, and all of a sudden we are having really interesting conversation[s], we're coming up with new, neat things.

Thus, the political space became displaced from the agora to ENGOs' and forestry companies' eighteen-month "conflict free period." Forestry companies agreed not to log or build roads in a list of valleys submitted by ENGOs,[4] so as to "maintain the full range of land use options in those key ecological areas identified in this Letter of Intent"; in turn, ENGOs agreed to "suspend" their international market campaign targeting the companies, so as to "maintain continuity of business/operations" (Joint Solutions Project 2000, 4). This was a serious agreement on behalf of forestry companies, which agreed not only to voluntarily withhold logging operations in the contentious areas but also to do so even in the face of pressure to log those areas. The ENGOs' side of the agreement was similarly substantial since the ENGOs had not only waged an effective market campaign to date but also had another prong of that campaign – a western red cedar campaign – ready to launch.[5]

The Letter of Intent also specified new relationships, thereby creating a new, hybrid group made up of former enemies that had chosen to work together to forge new solutions for land management in coastal British Columbia. Why had they chosen to work together? As the Letter of Intent states, "participating ENGOs and Companies both recognize the need to reconsider the approaches they have traditionally pursued with regards to issues/conflicts between them" (Joint Solutions Project 2000, 7). But what prompted this recognition? According to one environmentalist,

> it was a "Mexican standoff" ... It was just the point where everybody was all "okay, well, we can just all just keep doing what we're doing" [laughter] ... "or we could try to, kind of, invent a slightly different model here that, you know, takes a little bit from all of what we're doing."

The "Mexican standoff" model pits ecology against economy. It is a zero sum conflict. There is no possibility for movement since the two sides are evenly balanced. Recognition of this undesirable state of affairs was a key moment of transition for BC wilderness politics. Both sides agreed that they needed to "reconsider the approaches" that they had used up to that point. If these approaches can be characterized as the position taking in the agora and the maelstrom of bullets in the negotiating room, then we can say that these approaches helped to reproduce the modern constitution: the interests of conservation opposed the interests of development.

In contrast, the parties suggested the value of creating a new model. Importantly, this model would be developed by taking "a little bit from all of what we're doing." That is, the model was not to be imported from elsewhere, it was not about the imposition of one side on the other, it was not even about a balance, but it was about selecting elements from each party and articulating them together in a new network. This process began through an exchange of elements between ENGOs and forestry companies. Both sides had to give something up that was important to their identities. On the one side, "participating Companies acknowledge that cuts on the north and central coast will be coming down"; on the other, "participating ENGOs acknowledge that completion of an acceptable 'conservation-biology/ecosystem-based plan' will not necessarily require that all areas within the Standstill Arrangement be formally protected" (Joint Solutions Project 2000, 7). Once they had made these concessions, both parties agreed to accept an element from the other. "Participating Companies acknowledge that the Central and North Coast contains unique areas of forests and forest dwelling species (Kermode bear, Grizzly) and enjoys a global status in terms of environmental values," while "participating ENGOs recognize that Participating Companies have substantial degrees of investment at risk in this process and that sustainable forestry will continue to play a role in the region" (Joint Solutions Project 2000, 7, 8).

As a result of this new connection between them, participating ENGOs were no longer concerned solely about absolute protection of "pristine wilderness," and industry was no longer focused solely on maximal extraction of merchantable fibre. They were no longer "positions" firing rhetorical bullets at one another. Now participating ENGOs' interests included sustainable forestry, while the industry's interests included unique species and environmental values. ENGOs and forestry companies created a new hybrid entity formed out of environmentalist and industry interests.

This hybrid ENGO-forestry company group became a new obligatory point of passage for other interests in the coastal forests. Together, environmentalists and forestry companies defined other relevant groups, their interests, and how these interests should be met, as can be seen in the section of the Letter of Intent titled "Background" (in subsequent versions titled "Premises"):

1 Coastal forests of the north and central coast are ecologically significant in a local, regional, and global context.
2 The coastal forests of BC are the traditional territory of First Nations and are culturally, economically, environmentally and socially significant to the First Nations people of the coast.
3 This agreement is without prejudice to aboriginal rights and aboriginal title.
4 Coastal forests of [the] north and central coast are socially and economically significant in a local and regional context. (Joint Solutions Project 2000, 10)

Different (generic) groups of people at different local, regional, and global locations were recognized as having both ecological and economic interests in the forests. Luckily for them, the plan that ENGOs and industry were about to develop would help these groups to realize their interests. Additionally, the forests were recognized as being of special importance to First Nations, who had their own unique cultural, economic, environmental, and social interests. Luckily for them, the ENGO-industry agreement did not "prejudice ... aboriginal rights and title" and would thus not infringe on them. Moreover, not only would all of these different interests be met, but also they would be reconciled in the ENGO-industry conservation-biology/ecosystem-based plan, since, according to the Letter of Intent, "strong environmental protection, a strong economy, and a strong social fabric are directly linked" (Joint Solutions Project 2000, 10). Of course, the document implied that these interests would only be accommodated and reconciled if they went through the joint group's plan for the region. The plan thereby took over the centre of an emerging and evolving network.

Seeing People through the Trees

The conservation-biology/ecosystem-based plan proposed in the Letter of Intent was the result of environmentalists and forestry companies coming together in a new political space to forge common solutions. The first part of the plan came from ENGOs and their preference for conservation biology. The second part came from the forestry industry's experience with ecosystem-based management. The first focused on how to protect biodiversity from human use, the second on how to ensure that human use does not destroy ecosystems. Yet both would undergo change since a plan was created that focused on both ecological protection and forestry practice. In particular, the plan would tie forestry practice to biological conservation and tie both to "social, cultural and economic needs":

> With regards to the conservation/ecosystem planning component of the Planning Framework, Participating Companies and ENGOs will develop an approach to forest planning designed to achieve conservation of biodiversity as a primary forest management objective, and agree that a plan to do this must be based on the following core principles:
>
> (a) It must involve input from internationally recognized scientists and other relevant authorities.

(b) It must focus on protection of habitat for fish and wildlife.

(c) It must sustain natural forest characteristics.

(d) AAC [annual allowable cut] will be an output of planning, not an input.

(e) It must adopt a precautionary approach.

(f) It must involve adaptive management.

(g) It must be based on the use of harvesting techniques that emphasize low environmental impact and high timber value.

(h) It must address the social, cultural and economic needs of First Nations and local communities and provide a basis for economic stability and diversification. (Joint Solutions Project 2000, 11)

The solution presented did not purify the elements of the coastal forests into nature and society, for example by creating non-economic zones for protecting biodiversity from industrial development, on the one hand, and economic zones to support industrial development through forest management, on the other. Rather, the solution explicitly mixed humans and non-humans in an effort to "achieve conservation of biodiversity as a primary forest management objective." That is, forest management changed its focus from maximizing economic returns (within the "limits" of sustainability) to maximizing biodiversity while also maintaining extractive activities. Additionally, point (h) was a rather new one for both conservation biology and the ecosystem approach to forestry management. For example, the conservation area design reviewed in the previous chapter specifically excluded social, cultural, and economic issues to focus exclusively on biology and ecology. While acknowledging that "biodiversity may have economic and social values that are considerable and should be accounted for in management decisions," the authors of the CAD nevertheless suggested that it was more important to focus on the science first, which could thereafter be placed in the "hands of First Nations, local people, environmental organizations, forest industry, and government representatives" (Jeo et al. 1999, 18, 69). Indeed, the authors viewed this as a "particular strength of the CAD – it is a western science based statement made independent of specific economic or political interests" (12).

The conservation area design seeks to determine the facts free from the distorting influence of politics. It wants to speak only about nature, to shelter it from destructive human activities, to defend nature for nature's sake, and to describe the systems of nature as revealed through conservation biology (cf. Latour 2004, 20-21). However, according to one environmentalist, this attempt to purify science from politics and the natural from the social was a failing of the project:

Because we were a little slow and we weren't kind of, like, really all
over it [the CAD], we did the piece around "how do we do all the
ecological stuff? How do we put the things together for the grizzly
bears?" We didn't do the piece around "how do you talk to human
communities and figure out how everybody else fits in the picture?"
because we didn't have the skill sets, that wasn't who was in the room,
there were a lot us who were just scientists and pretty blinkered in
their vision.

This admission suggests that there are not two separate processes (science and politics) pertaining to two separate ontological realities (nature
and society) but a single "picture" made up of a heterogeneous list of actors
– ecological "stuff," grizzly bears, human communities, and "everybody
else." The conservation project thus cannot speak only about nature but
must take this heterogeneous association of beings into account: for example, one must "talk to human communities." The goal is not simply to
protect nature from people but also to figure out how everything and
everybody "fit" together. Moreover, given the large list of actors, it is not
clear for whose sake nature should be protected: can this project proceed
simply on the basis of the "intrinsic value" of biodiversity, or do other
values have to be taken into account? Finally, this project cannot be led
"only by scientists" who seek to uncover the systems of nature through
conservation biology; everything and everyone who are part of the picture
(or those who represent them) need to be "in the room."

While the conservation area design sought to define the conservation
requirements of the coastal forests as a "matter of fact," free from the
distorting bias of political, economic, social, or cultural considerations,
ENGOs and forestry companies together began to form what Latour (2004,
24) refers to as a *matter of concern;* in contrast to matters of fact, matters
of concern "have no clear boundaries, no well-defined essences, no sharp
separation between their own hard kernel and their environment." Matters
of concern are not out there waiting to be discovered by scientists but have
a historicity tied to their articulation by concerned parties. Thus, in the
conservation-biology/ecosystem-based plan described above, biodiversity
is not represented as an existing reality that can be maintained through
exclusion of particular forest uses. In contrast, the conservation of biodiversity is depicted as something that must be "achieved" through a plan.

There are other features of the plan that differentiate it from attempts
to define the "facts." The plan does not have clear boundaries but is situated in a network yet to be produced. This network is composed of things

such as "forest characteristics" and "habitat fish and wildlife," but also "AAC" (annual allowable cut) and "harvesting techniques" and "social, cultural and economic needs." It thus does not pertain to "the social or political world on one side and the world of objectivity and profitability on the other" (Latour 2004, 24). While this network will be investigated by "internationally recognized scientists and other relevant authorities," it will not be defined by them exclusively; rather, they are only one group who will provide "input," and the process of investigation will be open and controversial. Finally, in contrast to matters of fact, Latour (2004, 24) notes that "everyone paradoxically expects the unexpected consequences that [matters of concern] will not fail to produce – consequences that properly belong to them." The planning framework takes account of the inevitability of unexpected consequences with its specification of the need for a precautionary approach and adaptive management.

REVISING ENGOs' CONCEPTION OF WILDERNESS

It was a big shift for ENGOs to go from one position, where they dis-seminated scientific facts to try and protect nature from logging, to a second position, where they tried to balance conservation concerns with economic concerns. The original attempt to shift the BC environmental movement toward a comprehensive conservation strategy for the central and north coasts succeeded but at the cost of another, unexpected shift. Now that the ENGOs had the forestry companies right where they wanted them, under a giant hammer of the market campaign, the negotiators were engaging in a "love strategy," seeking to define joint solutions with industry! Here they had the chance and the "responsibility to all inhabit-ants of this planet, present and future, to set aside self-sustaining areas of temperate rainforest as wilderness, forever" (WCWC 1992), but one of the key negotiators was saying that "our ... basic conception of wilderness, that it's a place untouched by humans, is really wrong."[6]

This shift caused a big rift in the BC environmental movement (one that continues today) and the explosion of the Canadian Rainforest Network. As one environmentalist mentioned,

> so now we're in this, sort of, interesting solutions sort of realm with
> industry, and we're not yelling across the table at them ... Which is
> freaking a few people out because they're like, "okay, something's really
> screwy here, they are not supposed to be in bed together, they are *so*

not supposed to be in bed together." And, you know, people within the environmental movement are freaked out about it because they're going, "you guys are the sellouts," and it was all bad news.

According to one critical environmentalist, the negotiators "started suffering from Stockholm Syndrome," and as a result they lost their vision, which, "in a nutshell, is to protect all of the intact valleys in the Great Bear." Because of internal conflict associated with the negotiators' approach, "the Canadian Rainforest Network blew up, politics killed it." However, this led to the establishment of a new group, eventually known as the Rainforest Solutions Project (RSP):

> But what had happened as a result of all of that [internal conflict] was that we had sort of three or four individuals as part of that coalition who had really, really gotten to know each other well, had built trust together, had great working relationships, and wanted to keep working together because they were, like, "this is way more fun than working internally in our own individual organizations. We actually, like, there's zing here."

The four individuals – Merran Smith from Sierra BC, Tzeporah Berman from the Coastal Rainforest Coalition (soon to become ForestEthics), Karen Mahon of Greenpeace, and Jody Holmes of BC Wild – worked together to develop their own "vision" for the central and north coasts. This vision translated and developed one of the multiple and conflicting visions contained within the Canadian Rainforest Network. As noted in Chapter 2, this network recognized the need for economic opportunities on the central and north coasts, particularly for the communities there. This latter strand was developed in this new group's vision, as noted by an environmentalist interviewee:

> There was a year of kind of like the, there was no Canadian Rainforest Network, and there was no, sort of, what we now work for, which is the Rainforest Solutions Project, wherein, that group, that core group of good friends, basically all spent their time talking to big funders, saying, "we have this dream, we have this vision, of how it could be, and it's so different from anything we have ever done before 'cause we have to integrate people into it, we have to build conservation economies, there has to be money associated with this that is about taking care of the people, it's not just about protected areas, it's not just about

you get your big conservation wins, and you walk away from this, and then it basically falls apart."

The group was successful in obtaining $1 million from the Packard Foundation for this vision, more precisely defined as

> this network of protected areas and really amazing, sort of forest practices in the intervening spaces so that you really were maintaining ecological integrity over time. [And] a conservation economy that was looking after local communities where they were actually healthy and sane and able to take care of themselves and basically had self-governance. It was about that simple. Really, it wasn't any more complicated than that, it wasn't any more sophisticated than that at some level.

The plan might not have seemed very complicated or sophisticated; however, considering all the work that led up to it, it was no small feat. Both the coastal forests and environmentalists had undergone huge transformations. First there was the "forgotten coast" and indifferent environmentalists. Then there was the coastal temperate rainforest and interested environmentalists. Then there was the Great Bear Rainforest and an international coalition of environmentalists. Then there was the commodity chain and a major campaign win. Then the coalition blew up: the environmental movement was translated again, and so was the GBR. Now a small group of environmentalists shifted from attempts to close debate with the facts of nature to attempts to keep it open with a matter of concern. The land in question was no longer treated as a given, non-human reality that should be protected from humans; it was now an open question about how humans and non-humans should associate with one another. This was neither a simple transformation nor a simple task. Rather than attempting to protect something that already existed, environmentalists, together with their new forestry company allies, had to continue along the path of network formation. To do so, they had to convince others to accept the new roles that they had assigned for them.

RESISTING JOINT SOLUTIONS

According to Callon (1986), it is one thing to define (or "problematize") the interests and identities of elements that one wishes to associate in a network and another for those elements to accept such definitions and thereby become successfully "enrolled." This is not an easy task. Like the broader BC environmental movement, other groups criticized the new vision that was developing for the coastal forests. These groups contested the terms of their incorporation, particularly the fact that they were not "in the room" to represent their own interests. The ensuing controversy resulted in interesting processes of group formation and translation for local communities, First Nations, the provincial government, and the CFCI-ENGO group itself as these other actors sought to reject or transform the terms of the emerging network.

When they learned of the Letter of Intent (leaked to the news media), the Industrial Wood and Allied Workers of Canada (IWA), north island communities, First Nations, and the provincial government were very upset.[7] For example, "in a March 9 letter to Forests Minister Jim Doyle, the union says the deal would lead to 'the loss of employment for many IWA members and First Nations people who work in the area and the Lower Mainland'" (Hamilton 2000). Beyond concern about immediate impacts to employment, the primary criticism was that two unelected groups – ENGOs and forestry companies – were meeting "in secret" to make decisions about public and/or First Nations land (Hamilton 2000; Hume 2000; Lee 2000). One environmentalist admitted that, "in 2000, everybody was up in arms, because it was like, 'you guys are making decisions, you shouldn't be in control.' The government was just as pissed off at us as everybody else." According to the Union of British Columbia Mayors *Task Force Report on CFCI* (2000, 1), "it was particularly concerning that two parties, through closed-door negotiations, were attempting to make land use decisions on Crown land when a provincially sanctioned land use planning process was underway." In addition, a First Nations interviewee mentioned, "First Nations were not happy ... They saw this as being, again, meddling, with their rights and territories, who – no one was going to tell them how the forest was going to be managed."

These groups reacted to the creation of a new political space outside the LRMP. The latter was deemed to be legitimate and democratic, the former illegitimate and "secret." However, from the perspectives of environmentalists and forestry companies, the agora of the LRMP made it impossible to experiment with new approaches to land-use governance. Thus, their focus was not to create plans in secret but to provide a new political space that included others. In other words, they endeavoured to recreate politics in order to shift from the modern constitution to the collective. Different groups had different reactions to this goal.

The provincial government responded by stating in a letter dated May 19, 2000 (quoted in UBCM Task Force on CFCI 2000, 3), that the "government's role in this issue is to ensure an open democratic decision process that will protect markets, communities, and the environment" and that the government "cannot endorse a process that does not include all stakeholders, particularly First Nations." However, the letter did suggest at least tacit support for the process, which it recognized as being the result of ENGOs' market campaign in combination with a slow LRMP process (MacLennan 2000), stating that the "government, however, is prepared to assist the parties in further discussions that would result in their returning to the LRMP table" (UBCM Task Force on CFCI 2000, 3). A comment made by Graem Wells, chair of the CCLRMP, represents the government's perspective:

> In order for the CFCI/ENGO initiative to work, there needs to be buy-in from all the parties. The model that has been discussed in terms of the Central Coast LRMP being the parent of this process and the place where land use decisions are made, is the proper one in his view. The technical and scientific work needs to be a subset of the LRMP process. (summarized in Dovetail Consulting 2000c, 7)

Forestry workers and north island mayors were more confrontational, going so far as attempting to launch a short-lived counter-campaign termed "Operation Defend."[8] As stated in an op-ed in the *Courier-Islander* (MacLennan, 2000), "the Truck Loggers Association has an interesting idea. They are proposing to start a public relations battle in support of B.C. forest products and in opposition of the Coast Forest Conservation Initiative (CFCI)." A workshop organized by Port McNeil mayor Gerry Furney was held in support of this initiative on September 22, 2000. According to the Western Canada Wilderness Committee (2000), "an August 24, 2000 information package was mailed to various B.C. mayors, councillors, and community leaders asking them to join together to fight the 'current campaign by the extremist enviro-elite.'"

The response of First Nations was captured by a sentiment expressed by Caunie Saunders of the Nuxalk First Nation:

> First Nations are not involved in the direct planning; nor are they provided meaningful consultation. The Nuxalk Nation cannot support the CFCI/ENGO initiative without full participation of First Nations throughout the planning stages. Going behind closed doors to negotiate agreements

between industry and environmental groups was not acceptable ... First
Nations want to be involved directly in the planning process. (summarized
in Dovetail Consulting 2000c, 7)

Similarly, Dallas Smith of the Kwakiutl Laich-Kwil-Tach Nations Society
stated that

the basic principle of justice for First Nations in their territories needs
to be honoured through meaningful involvement in land use and management ... There are lessons to be learned from First Nations about finding
solutions to the current conflicts and resource scarcities, problems that
the First Nations did not create. (summarized in Dovetail Consulting
2000c, 7)

The reaction of the provincial government was to try to fold the initiative
back into the LRMP, but this was unlikely for all the reasons given above.
The reaction of local communities in the form of Operation Defend was
to destroy the initiative by launching a public relations campaign against
environmentalists. This was unlikely as well since environmentalists
had already enrolled the international market and forestry companies in
their project. Reactions from First Nations were different. They had also
boycotted the LRMP and were thus less concerned about the affront to
democracy that the initiative represented. For First Nations, this was a
problematic democracy that recognized them merely as one stakeholder
among many. Their central concern was recognition of their right to make
decisions about and benefit from uses of their traditional territories. For
them, it didn't really matter which table was discussing land use; what
mattered was to be at that table making decisions.

In fact, the development of a potentially new political space provided
First Nations with an opportunity to engage more fully in decisions about
their territories. To make this possibility a reality, leaders of First Nations
on the central and north coasts and Haida Gwaii (Queen Charlotte Islands)
came together at five meetings throughout 2000[9] in order to forge a coast-
wide group called the Turning Point Initiative (subsequently Coastal First
Nations). The purpose of the group was to address common issues, such
as unemployment and lack of access to resources in traditional territories.
More importantly, the group was established to ensure that First Nations
were "in the room" in which land-use planning was taking place.[10] One
First Nations interviewee indicated that

our first task, when we came together, was to recognize that we aren't in a room, and we better position ourselves to get into a particular room that met our kind of interest better. And, to that end, we had a series of bilateral meetings with forest company presidents, with the Truck/Loggers Association, with the union, and with the enviros, all bilaterals. [We] just said, "Look it, we have some interests here, and we want to hear what your interests are and see if we can come together."

This process was facilitated by the ENGO-forestry industry obligatory passage point. But it meant that First Nations' interests were transformed by the encounter. Identities were relational. Local communities strengthened their identities in opposition to the initiative (with Operation Defend), and the provincial government tried to maintain its identity as the legitimate forum for political decision making. First Nations, for their part, used the opportunity to strengthen an aspect of their identities by creating a unified group to engage with other interests.

Moreover, the furor surrounding the environmentalists and forest companies' discussions prompted important changes to the nascent ENGO-CFCI group's makeup, process, and self-definition. The CFCI lost two of its members when West Fraser Timber announced that it was selling its coastal tenures and Interfor announced that it was leaving the group to deal directly with customers and stakeholders. In turn, this prompted Greenpeace to leave the group in order to re-establish its campaign against Interfor, which included familiar tactics such as climbing on top of equipment and unfurling a banner at Interfor's Fraser Valley sawmill (Stueck 2000). According to Linda Coady, Vice President, Environmental Enterprise, Weyerhaeuser BC Coasta Group (2002, 36), "maintaining internal social license necessary to maintain the cease-fire agreement (i.e. conflict-free period) became very difficult once splits emerged in both caucuses and some companies and ENGOs exited the alliance and began to challenge it." However, the strength of the hybrid coalition was demonstrated by the resolve of the remaining ENGOs and forestry companies to continue their project and by efforts on both sides to bring Interfor and Greenpeace back into the group (CFCI 2001; Sierra Club, Coastal Rainforest Coalition, and Rainforest Action Network 2001). Moreover, one company representative noted, the backlash actually served to *strengthen* the coalition:

This was probably the first time – all of a sudden the companies and the ENGOs actually had an issue where they had more in common than they didn't. [The backlash] represented a common threat to both of them for different reasons ... Because, for the companies, if they couldn't contain it, they knew that they were going to lose customers. And, for the ENGOs, if they couldn't contain it, they saw that they were going to possibly lose this progress that they just [made] ... And so this is where they actually, for the first time, began to collaborate around an issue.

From Technical Expertise to Collaborative Research

In response to the backlash, the ENGO-CFCI group began to carefully specify its identity as a "technical and scientific resource" rather than as a decision-making body (Dovetail Consulting 2000a, 5). For example, in a workshop,

> Linda [Coady] stated that the companies and environmental organizations involved in the initiative fully recognize that they are not the decision makers with respect to land use on the Central and North Coast of BC, but hope that whatever information or ideas that they are able to put together may help inform the decisions that lie ahead for other groups. (Dovetail Consulting 2000c, 3)

Although this framing tends toward the reproduction of a distinction between science and politics (similar in form to the distinction made in the conservation area design), at this point ENGOs and forestry companies were just two groups among several others now gathered around a common matter of concern.

Indeed, the ENGO-CFCI group positioned itself as a simple "resource," not only to assuage fears that they were making decisions behind closed doors, but also because they no longer had control over the issue and were thus forced to take a tangent. Recognizing that they could not "go ahead without the support of the other groups," the ENGO-CFCI decided to "start again and change the direction" (Coady, cited in Hamilton 2000). Their encounters with other groups thus prompted a translation of their project. In a joint release dated May 29, 2000, ENGOs and the CFCI apologized for creating concerns and said that they would spend the next sixty days consulting

> with affected logging contractors, workers, and communities to demonstrate how new approaches to ecosystem planning and conservation-based manage-

ment can address the interests of all those with a stake in coastal forests, [in addition to working] with the provincial government and the Central Coast LRMP to develop a mechanism to link this initiative to the provincial land use planning framework. (cited in UBCM Task Force on CFCI 2000, 5)

In so doing, the ENGO-CFCI opened up the matter of concern even further. Matters of fact are supposed to be discovered by experts; other groups can later debate what to do about their consequences. In contrast, matters of concern involve multiple groups, expert and lay, in the articulation of states of affairs. Criticism of an over-reliance on experts was made in a series of workshops convened to consult with others (Dovetail Consulting 2000a, 7; 2000b, 3; 2000c). For example, in one of the workshops,

> several participants spoke forcefully about their unease over reliance on experts. Based on their experience at the community level, empowerment and building on local skills and expertise is often a more successful approach. As one person put it, "instead of going to experts, I say, go back into the community and then you get a real genuine mandate ... The keys are in the communities and not necessarily with the experts!" (Dovetail Consulting 2000a, 9)

This was not to say that participants saw no value in science, however, or that they wanted to exclude science from these processes. Rather, the emphasis was on integrating different ways of taking things into account. Reinforcing similar points made by others,

> one participant commented that the essential thing, along with being inclusive of all interests involved, is to have a collaborative research process established between the community development interests and the researchers. Local practitioners will need to engage with researchers to frame the appropriate questions, rather than trying to establish priorities in advance: "If we want to brainstorm deliverables, fine; but defining the nature of the problem has to be done collaboratively through participatory action research." (Dovetail Consulting 2000b, 28)

The sentiments captured in these excerpts express dissatisfaction with the view that a select group of experts alone can determine the facts. Rather, all groups who have an interest in the issue must be involved in a "collaborative research process." When experts "establish priorities in advance," other groups are disempowered. Not only are their unique skills and knowledge not drawn on, but also research projects fail to "frame the appropriate questions." This sentiment disrupts the fact/value distinction associated with the modern constitution.

In modernity, facts and values were to remain as separate as possible (Latour 2004, 95). Various interest groups could debate their interests in political forums, but scientists alone had the capacity for a "double rupture." Drawing on Plato's allegory of the cave, Latour (2004, 10) argues that under the first rupture "the Philosopher, and later the Scientist, have to free themselves of the tyranny of the social dimension, public life, politics, subjective feelings, popular agitation – in short from the dark of the Cave – if they want to accede to truth." However, under the second rupture,

> the Scientist, once equipped with laws not made by human hands that he has just contemplated because he has succeeded in freeing himself from the prison of the social world, can go back into the Cave so as to bring order to it with incontestable findings that will silence the endless chatter of the ignorant mob. (11)

As a result, experts "can make the mute world speak, tell the truth without being challenged [and] put an end to the interminable arguments through an incontestable form of authority that would stem from the things themselves" (14). The groups consulted by the ENGO-CFCI challenged this model. They did not want the experts to go out and determine facts that would tell people what they had to do. They did not suggest that everything should be left to political debate. Rather, they wanted to make sure that all relevant interests were involved in framing "appropriate" questions in collaborative research. Relevance, appropriateness, and research were folded together in a way that blended facts and values. Rather than leaving determination of the common world up to experts and determination of the common good up to non-experts in a public debate, they came to "take the question of the common good and that of the common world, values and facts, as a single, identical goal" (Latour 2004, 94).

Latour (2004) suggests that the distinction between facts and values that supports the modern constitution can be replaced with another distinction that can support the collective – one between "taking into account" and "putting in order." Rather than maintaining a divide between science and politics, as in the modern constitution, all interested groups are involved in both processes. In the first, interested parties work together to examine, research, and explore the common matter of concern that has their interest. In the second, the same parties find ways to reconcile the various elements in the world that they are collectively constructing. The period of consultation engaged in by the ENGO-CFCI brought to light other groups' (particularly First Nations') desires for a collective taking into account of the elements to be part of the matter of concern.

TRANSLATING THE VISION

As a result of demands made by groups consulted, the ENGO-CFCI (hereafter referred to as the Joint Solutions Project, or JSP, as it had been renamed by this point) was forced to admit other interests into their plan and, accordingly, release exclusive control over that plan. Thus, the matter of concern *itself* began to undergo transformation. At a series of meetings collectively referred to as the Meetings at the Met,[11] the plan, according to one environmentalist interviewed, began to develop "additional dimensions to it and additional, kind of, meaning to it." For example, while ENGOs' campaigns and the Letter of Intent mentioned First Nations and their interests, "our original vision didn't have a strong piece for First Nations ... They came, and their vision was control." In order for First Nations to become enrolled in the network, their interests had to be taken into account and articulated with the framework that ENGOs and forestry companies were developing. Not only did this influence the framework, but also it influenced First Nations' relationships with other groups, including the provincial government, and their role in land-use planning. As one company representative suggested,

> I think one of the most significant things that came out of those meetings was that a decision had been taken internally within JSP where part of their message was that the purpose of the LRMPs and the purpose of these negotiations were to come up with recommendations that could then be dealt with in [a First Nations] government-to-[provincial] government context.

From the perspective of ENGOs, this process involved the addition of a number of different interests to their interest in conservation. As one of the environmentalists noted, "we had our conservation vision at the core, and then we added on [support for] government-to-government [negotiations], which is what First Nations wanted, and worker transition, which is what industry needed and the communities needed, and dah, dah, dah."

However, while the interests were different, it was possible to articulate them: "It was a matter of sewing together, finding the thread to bring all those visions together." And EBM was this thread: "We were all on the same EBM page, even though they were slightly different EBMs. You know, whatever, you look back, and you go, 'oh, my god, what craziness that people couldn't get over themselves.' But it didn't matter because everybody was talking EBM, with their slight nuances." Yet, since "everybody was talking EBM," no single group in particular "owned" this matter of concern. Now that other groups started to become enrolled, ENGOs had to give up further ownership of the vision and allow it to develop in relation to the new elements: "You have to let go of the vision, and it has to not be yours anymore," one environmentalist mentioned, "for everyone else to own it – [and] they need to own it – which means you have to let go of it." The matter of concern developed, shifted, and changed as groups, which themselves shifted and changed, became connected to it. No one group owned the matter of concern or had an expert view. All groups brought a little of what they were doing, to paraphrase the quotation presented earlier, in order to create a new model for conservation and development in coastal British Columbia, one "sewn together" by EBM.

The shift from the modern constitution to the collective involves a shift in forms of authority and responsibility. Instead of scientists, who act as spokespersons for the facts, and politicians, who act as spokespersons for values, multiple groups contribute their skills in the single construction site of the collective (Latour 2004, 137). JSP took politicians' authority away by creating an alternative political space. At the same time, other groups were quick to make sure that the JSP did not become an exclusive form of alternative authority. These groups also served to take authority away from scientific experts by arguing for the inclusion of all interested parties in the research project. Accordingly, the roles of scientists, politicians, and others were displaced and rearticulated. Scientists were not excluded but now seen as collaborators. Likewise, the provincial government was decentred but not ignored. Rather, it came to take on a new role.

The government was enrolled to put its stamp of legitimacy on the decisions, even though these had largely been made outside of government-sanctioned processes. For this to take place, the various elements of the project produced thus far were inserted into government procedures – the CCLRMP – and repackaged there. First, of the JSP's list of valleys that would not be developed during negotiations, twenty were designated as new candidate "protection areas," while the remaining seventy-seven were designated as "option areas," meaning that future negotiations would determine their status. Other valleys agreed in the Letter of Intent for conflict-free harvesting were designated as "operating areas." Second, the CCLRMP adopted the JSP's EBM framework for future planning in the CCLRMP. Third, the CCLRMP adopted the JSP's plans for dealing with economic change, including provisions for short-term compensation and mitigation[12] and medium- and long-term plans to establish a Coast Development Trust, to be funded by provincial and federal governments as well as ENGOs and forestry companies, with the purpose of "enabling socio-economic change." And fourth, the CCLRMP adopted the JSP's draft terms of reference for an assessment team to develop EBM and recommend how it should be applied to the coast.

With these elements of the emerging matter of concern now repackaged, the government announced, with much fanfare, a new interim agreement for the central coast on April 4, 2001. On the same day, the government and eight First Nations belonging to the Turning Point coalition signed a General Protocol Agreement on Land Use Planning and Interim Measures.[13] Among other things, the agreement explicitly elevated First Nations from "stakeholders" to "governments" with special rights and responsibilities. For example, the agreement states that, "where the Province intends to undertake a land use planning process in a designated geographic area, the Province will work with First Nations to define principles, anticipated scope and outcomes of the land use planning process" (2). Moreover, the agreement states that, "where a First Nation(s) cannot agree to a recommendation(s) from the inclusive planning forum, a government-to-government process will be established to attempt to resolve the outstanding matter(s) directly with the Province of British Columbia" (3). The protocol agreement also committed each party to developing its own land-use plan with guidance from the EBM framework included in the framework agreement.

ENGOs were forced to relinquish control over their vision for the coastal forests as a result of the enrolment of forestry companies and, later, First Nations. Blending their interests and identities with those of forestry companies in the Joint Solutions Project, ENGOs were transformed (taking on the identity of the Rainforest Solutions Project). So too were forestry companies (now the Coast Forest Conservation Initiative) and First Nations (now Turning Point – Coastal First Nations). With these groups so convened, the vision shifted from one of absolute protection on the basis of biological necessity – which maintained a separation between nature and society – to one of ecological protection, forestry reform, and economic development. How the transformed matter of concern was to be achieved (i.e., turned into a fact) was a key topic of debate and negotiation, and it became formatted under the rubric of EBM. EBM became the container that articulated disparate interests, as well as the promise that they could become commensurate. This meant that the obligatory point of passage could not position itself as a form of scientific authority separate from the political process but only as an open process of research engaged in by all relevant parties – a process of research in which values would be considered alongside facts. It is to this process of engaged research and experimentation that I now turn.

4

Mobilizing Allies and
Reconciling Interests

As elements are drawn into a network, they undergo a series of transformations. They are "mobilized" from their original locations and
brought to a new centre where they are articulated and combined (Callon
1986). The ensuing network performs its reality through the contributions
of its elements, each defined in relation to all the others. Previous chapters
focused on the chains of translation involved in defining, interesting, and
enrolling groups in the emerging GBR network. This analysis traced the
performance of the GBR as a globally significant ecosystem capable of
supporting the livelihood of rights holding First Nations and a significantly
reformed forestry sector. However, the performance at this stage was
only tentative and provisional. Elements had been assembled and conceptually contained but not yet well articulated. A key tension remained
between conservation and economy – traditionally opposed performances
pertaining to unique networks. While the process of network formation
was heterogeneous and involved many translations of identities and interests, ENGOs nevertheless attempted to conceptually sever the network
into nature and society. However, now that the vision itself began to shift
and change, this process of purification began to give way to a process of
composition. This chapter focuses specifically on the procedures through
which groups' interests were reconciled into one common world.

Although I showed how this process constructed the (hybrid) reality of
the coastal forests, this is a very different analysis from one that would be
applied by a *social* constructionist. Social constructionist analysts of British
Columbia's war in the woods argue that the conflict rested on a paradigm

that pitted trees against jobs, conservation against development, and society against nature (Doyle, Elliott, and Tindall 2000; Rossiter 2004; Sandilands 2002; Stefanick 2001; Willems-Braun 1997). For example, Rossiter (2004, 142) argues that Greenpeace's GBR campaign materials "visually and discursively constructed a concept of pristine nature" by highlighting the age and aesthetic majesty of old-growth forests in photos and accompanying texts. As a result, argues Rossiter, "the nature Greenpeace sets out to protect leaves no room for human economy, technology, or politics" (151-52).

Social constructionist writers thus analyze conflict over BC forests as one of competing frames, a "struggle over meanings" (Sandilands 2002, 140) that constructs nature and society in dualistic terms – a problem that should be "overcome." As Stefanick (2001, 64, 67) writes, wilderness conflict in British Columbia "is in large part due to the divergent frames of British Columbia's forests," so "efforts must be made to overcome the assumption within both frames that there exists a dualism with respect to the human condition and the state of nature." Similarly, Rossiter (2004, 161) suggests that analyses such as his "should help to move us beyond the nature versus culture dualism that has permeated so much of the 'war in the woods' and encourage debate as to the kind of nature(s) that we would like to inhabit in the future." For his part, Willems-Braun (1997, 25) argues for constructions that place "in question those representations that construct nature as external to cultural and social relations."

Largely, these writers set out to debunk the false claims about forests put out by environmentalists and forestry companies. British Columbia's forests are not really either "pristine wilderness" or "natural resources." These are just social constructions imposed on forests and other people – particularly First Nations – who view forests in very different ways. If we want to make room for these other constructions, they argue, then we have to "overcome" the human/nature dualism that forecloses the possibility of seeing nature in connection with cultural and social relations. However, a consequence of analyzing the "cultural logic" behind this dualism – that is, as the outcome of "representational practices," "frames," and "struggles over meaning" – is to restrict political responses. Social constructionists generally do not claim that reality is comprised solely of representations; rather, they analyze the representations at play while withholding ontological claims about the reality so represented (Burningham and Cooper 1999). This is highly valuable work. However, in choosing not to account for the simultaneously material and discursive channels through which representation emerges, social constructionists can leave readers with little sense of how to respond. How can actors escape a social construction, other than by creating an alternative social construction? That is, while Rossiter (2004, 161) suggests that we should debate which kinds of nature we want to inhabit, it is unclear what these natures would look like, other than as "concepts" that have "emerged through social, political and economic interactions." But how does one inhabit a concept? The actors remain trapped in "cultural and social relations" that have little contact with non-humans, other than in thought.

To avoid this "pitfall of 'social representations' of nature," Latour (2004, 32) suggests that it is best to follow the world-building activities of the actors themselves. This entails that we look at more than their representational practices. In its campaign materials, Greenpeace did use words such as *ancient* and *pristine*. But does this mean that it thereby constructed a nature that "leaves no room for human economy, technology, or politics?" (Rossiter 2004, 151-52). Environmental conflicts are not only conflicts of words, rhetoric, argument, policy, or civil disobedience but also involve the mobilization of heterogeneous human and non-human elements. When we locate representations in panoramas that circulate in networks, as I did in Chapter 2, we can see that representations do material work. Moreover, we are free to explore how this work fits into an overall project that seeks to avoid dualisms between nature and society, trees and jobs, conservation and development.

FINDING AN OCCASION TO LINK ECOLOGICAL INTEGRITY AND HUMAN WELL-BEING

EBM formed the heart of the matter of concern linking scientists, ENGOs, forestry companies, First Nations, local communities, and the provincial government, but it remained vaguely defined. While everyone was talking EBM, they were still uncertain what it was, other than a list of philosophical principles that mixed humans and non-humans in surprising configurations. This uncertainty about EBM was suggested by a forestry industry interviewee:

> To me, ecosystem-based management is very easy to understand, and it is "have we compromised the functioning of the ecosystem?" If the answer is "no," then it really doesn't matter what extraction has taken place, because it means that we must have replaced the quantity and

the quality with something else, and it would be the same quality and the same quantity – this is a very confusing way of saying it – but the point is it's not just the exploitive, extractive model, but rather it's understanding the ecosystem function … And that's what we are trying to do with EBM, philosophically. And, of course, the complex thing is turning that into a reality, and what does that actually mean when you are on the ground, and that's the complicated part.

Even the high-level, philosophical understanding of EBM, which might seem "very easy to understand" in the mind of someone very close to it, becomes "confused" when it is translated into an explanation. How much more "complex" and "complicated" it must be to translate it "on the ground"! Latour (2004, 83) refers to uncertain associations of humans and non-humans as "propositions" to indicate their difference from a "statement" that either does or does not correspond to the reality that it seeks to represent. According to Latour (1999, 141), propositions are "*occasions* given to different entities to enter into contact. These occasions for interaction allow the entities to modify their definitions over the course of an event."[1] In the case of the GBR, the interests of bears, trees, salmon, environmentalists, forestry companies, and First Nations (among others) could now be brought into contact through the "occasion" offered by EBM. Indeed, according to another participant, EBM is

> just a euphemism that provides an effective vehicle for people to have
> quite useful discussions about what their interests are and how can
> they, sort of, broker relationships and understandings that don't under-
> mine those interests. That's why ecosystem-based management in the
> central and north coasts has taken quite a different flavour than you
> would normally attribute to it, just from reading the literature and
> stuff, and why it now clearly has the socio-economic element to it
> but also the governance element to it.

However, EBM at this point only offered an "occasion" for these interests to come "into contact" with one another. "Relationships and understandings" still needed to be "brokered" in a manner that reconciled these interests without "undermining" them. A great deal of work lay ahead to articulate these interests with one another.[2]

The first venue for this "on the ground" work was in the territories of two First Nations. In April 2001, about the same time as the announcement of the framework agreement, the Gitga'at and Kitasoo First Nations convened meetings with ENGOs and forestry companies to discuss land use in their traditional territories. These negotiations resulted in a protocol signed by hereditary and elected chiefs of the First Nations, representatives of the forestry companies, and ENGOs. Subsequent to the agreement, the parties formed the Kitasoo-Gitga'at Protocol Implementation Team, or Kit-Git-Pit. According to one participant,

> it [the Kit-Git-Pit] was really pivotal in that it was kind of like the "on the ground" way of modelling a bunch of the ideas that are great in principle and theory, but you have to really check that it was going to work. And it was basically the progenitor of the *EBM Handbook* – it created the *EBM Handbook*. And I think the other piece that it created really beautifully was this idea of needing to get a new governance structure. And also the idea that we need to pilot this idea of conservation financing.

The three "pieces" developed by the Kit-Git-Pit – the *EBM Handbook,* conservation financing, and a new governance structure – were the key mechanisms for reconciling conservation, development, and justice in the GBR, and thus the Kit-Git-Pit was "really where we drove the whole thing."

The Kit-Git-Pit produced the first drafts of the *EBM Handbook.* Eventually, the handbook was released under the auspices of the Coast Information Team, accorded the legitimacy of "an independent advisory body bring[ing] together the best available scientific, technical, traditional, and local knowledge" (Cardinal 2004, 1). The *EBM Handbook* became a central document, forming the touchstone of the GBR network. In particular, the document was accorded essential status for the full implementation of EBM by March 31, 2009, on which the agreement hinged. For example, in its document entitled *Definition of Full Implementation of EBM by March 31, 2009,* the Joint Land and Resource Forums (2007, 1) defined EBM as "an adaptive, systematic approach to managing human activities, *guided by the Coast Information Team EBM Handbook,* that seeks to ensure the co-existence of healthy, fully functioning ecosystems and human communities" (emphasis added).

The handbook is particularly important because it inscribes the processes of articulating the proposition that petitions the network convened to consider it: ecologically significant First Nations' territories or, as the handbook puts it, ecological integrity and human well-being. With the concept of "assessment," the handbook draws attention to things that need to be taken into account to articulate EBM and who is best to judge them:

"Assessment refers to the range of ecological, biophysical, cultural, and socio-economic inventory and analysis that is carried out to develop information needed to engage in design, integration, and implementation at various planning scales, and also to monitor the outcomes of management activity" (Cardinal 2004, 19). Lest one considers that the task of assessment is to be exclusively engaged in by scientists, or that assessment refers to separate tasks (scientific, cultural, and socio-economic) applied to separate spheres (nature, culture, and society), the principle of "collaboration" (detailed in section 2.4.9 of the handbook) ensures that they are assessed in an inclusive and integrated manner:

> EBM planning should engage people – First Nations, senior governments, resource users, tenure holders, local communities, and local people – meaningfully in developing and implementing plans as necessary at all scales. Collaboration provides a means for affected parties to establish interests, objectives, constraints, and incentives to ensure that land use and resource development supports community well-being. (Cardinal 2004, 15)

Here the focus is not on having scientists determine the ecological "facts" that might then be presented to politicians so that they can make decisions. Rather, everyone/thing that has a stake in the articulation of EBM is represented and has a voice in how it should be investigated and judged. Scientists, together with their trees and animals, can investigate the ecological integrity of the region. First Nations, with their members, elders, and consultants, can investigate the cultural features of the landscape. Local people in need of employment (primarily First Nations), together with their communities, economic development experts, and local entrepreneurs, can assess the prospects for economic development in the region.

Non-humans are given voice through the same filters encountered in Chapter 2. Given the sheer numbers and complex relationships among non-humans in the coastal forests, representatives must be found to stand in for them. According to the Coast Information Team (CIT), "coarse filter approaches to maintaining ecological integrity acknowledge that there are myriad species about which we know little or nothing, and that our ability to predict ecosystem processes is, at best, very limited" (Holt et al. 2004, 28). These strategies designate representative ecosystems,[3] which are defined as "ecosystems that are especially common, that define the character of a region" (Cardinal 2004, 75).[4]

Similarly, human communities are considered to be complex and difficult to understand. According to the *EBM Handbook,*

> socio-economic planning is also most likely to be successful when it treats people and their communities as living systems; as communities, sectors, and constituencies whose relationships are as significant as their individual needs and interests; who behave and respond in creative and unpredictable ways; who need to learn and adapt in order to be successful. (Cardinal 2004, 7)

In this definition, the principle of symmetry is in play: non-humans and humans are taken into account in similar ways, since both are understood as living, unpredictable, adaptive systems defined by their relationships. Moreover, both ecological integrity and human well-being are complex and difficult to understand. It is for this reason that representatives are chosen.

We can start to trace the ways in which the actors worked to construct a world that avoided the ideas that nature and society already exist in themselves and that the purpose of conservation projects is to find acceptable trade-offs between them that would result in some balance. As argued in the EBM framework, the

> idea of entrenching a demand for both human wellbeing and ecosystem integrity veers sharply away from thinking in terms of a "trade-off" between people and the environment. Obviously, any practical application has hundreds of small trade-offs: between interests, between components of the ecosystem, across time, and across space. However, ultimately, maintenance of ecological integrity and improvement of human wellbeing are critical; maintaining or improving one at the expense of the other is unacceptable because either way the foundation of life is undermined. (Aikman et al. 2004, 3)

Indeed, even the idea of finding a "balance" between conservation and development, central to ideas of sustainable development (Brundtland 1987), is replaced. As one environmentalist interviewee put it,

> *balance* is the wrong word, that's actually probably the issue: the interest was ecological conservation/sustainability with human well-being ensured throughout it. Now, the truth was that we didn't envision that

we were going to balance those two – that is, trade-off ecological sustainability for human well-being ... My vision would be that, while ...
maintaining ecological integrity of the area, you would find ways to
secure human well-being that may be different from current options,
economic options. For example, you don't just say, "okay, we're gonna
go log because we have to maintain human well-being."

This way of understanding the relationship between ecological integrity
and human well-being is also contained in the *EBM Handbook:*

> The goal to maintain ecological integrity defines an overarching context for
> achieving high levels of human well-being, primarily because it implies a
> commitment to sustainable, cautious resource use. However, this does not
> necessarily limit community and business development. EBM also implies
> negotiation of new arrangements through which First Nations, communities,
> and businesses collaborate to find innovative ways of implementing manage-
> ment and achieving development. (Cardinal 2004, 5)

The "new arrangements" are key. If one begins with the assumption that
society and nature are separate spheres, and that the interests of ecological
conservation and economic development are inherently opposed, then the
best that one can strive for is a balance involving the least worst set of
trade-offs. However, if one denies the premise and instead says that we
can create worlds in which we would like to live, then conservation and
development can be reconciled. But this requires the development of
specific mechanisms and arrangements to achieve the mutual accommo-
dation. That is, both the sphere of ecology and the sphere of economy
need to undergo changes if they are to relate to one another in positive
sum rather than zero sum terms.

EBM: Rendering Ecology Commensurable with Economy

In the *EBM Handbook,* four specific procedures are applied to the sphere
of ecology to render it commensurable with the sphere of economy: variation, risk, scale, and time. First, the handbook draws on recent ecological
research recognizing that ecosystems are not static but dynamic entities
characterized by a certain degree of disturbance. As noted in the handbook's
support document, *The Scientific Basis of EBM* (Holt et al. 2004, 13-14),
"implicit in the *Handbook* is the understanding that the reference point

against which ecological integrity is measured is the ecosystem as defined by natural disturbance processes." The document notes later that "natural disturbances, along with the activities of First Nations peoples, have historically shaped the composition and structure of forests on the coastal landscape. A good understanding of natural disturbance dynamics is an important first step towards maintaining ecosystem function and habitat characteristics to which native species have adapted" (17). As the document notes, a number of elements render the coastal forests variable by inducing disturbance. Wind, fires, insects, animals, floods, avalanches, extreme weather events: all of these things can destroy trees and open the forest canopy. Moreover, the "return interval," or the time that it takes for the forest to re-establish itself after disturbance, is measured on the scale of millennia. However, disturbance regimes for the coastal forests, as noted in the document, are small and infrequent (Holt et al. 2004, 17). This "range of natural variation," as it is called, is then taken as the benchmark for ecological integrity. Thus, ecological integrity is not a static entity but is viewed as the outcome of a number of processes – human and non-human (though the role of First Nations in producing disturbance is not discussed in the document) – that produce a particular range.

This is far from the "pristine wilderness" concept deployed during the war in the woods. Rather than viewing the forests as pure, such that any human use would entail a desecration, they are viewed as variable and thus in principle able to incorporate human use as one form of disturbance among many. Nevertheless, the bounds of this disturbance are tightly delimited, given the minor and infrequent nature of disturbance events in the coastal forests. More precisely, the integration of human activity into ecological integrity is determined by the concept of the risk threshold, the second procedure used to transform ecology in order to render it commensurable with economy.

According to the concept of the risk threshold, "low risk begins at the threshold where adverse impacts begin to be detected, and the transition to high risk corresponds to where significant loss of ecological function is expected to occur" (Cardinal 2004, 10). The Coast Information Team determined that reducing the amount of old-growth trees in an ecosystem by 30 percent is a low or precautionary risk threshold, while reducing trees by 70 percent is a high risk threshold.[5] According to the *EBM Handbook,* multiplication of the range of natural variation by low and high risk thresholds yields precautionary and high risk management targets. Thus, for example, if the range of natural variation of a particular ecosystem entails that 85-93 percent of it will contain old-growth trees, multiplying this range by low and high risk thresholds yields a precautionary range of old-growth trees at 59-65 percent and a high risk range of 25-28 percent (Cardinal 2004, 11).

Although the primary goal is to ensure low risk to ecological integrity, room for manoeuvre is built in by articulating risk with scale and time, the third and fourth procedures used in the *EBM Handbook.* The handbook differentiates the central and north coasts into a hierarchy of scales, with the "sub-region" or "sub-territory" defining the highest scale, then decreasing in a nested series through "landscape," "watershed," and "site" or "stand." Rather than protecting the region in one giant park, protection is to be applied to particularly sensitive landscapes at a variety of scales, leaving the intervening spaces for other uses. At the highest (regional) level, "representative ecosystems" might be given protected status. The intervening spaces do not have legislated protected status but protect important ecological, First Nations', and recreation values in reserves at the landscape level and in stand retention at the site level.

Low-risk activities are required in protected areas, reserves, and stand retention areas. However, higher-risk activities are deemed acceptable at lower scales with lower conservation values as long as the risk averages out to low at the highest level, since "the underlying assumption is that it is not necessary to sustain all species and processes everywhere all the time in order to maintain ecological integrity, as long as lower risk management objectives and targets are being achieved at strategic subregional and landscape planning scales" (Cardinal 2004, 11).

Time is also an important dimension with respect to risk. Although the overall goal is low risk across all ecosystem types, the actors recognize that this goal does not need to be achieved immediately. Rather, it is a long-term goal to be achieved by a plan, thus enabling flexibility and variability on the way to its successful institution. As noted by one company representative,

> where all the parties are at now, at least CFCI and RSP, is that by March 31, 2009, there will be a system in place, and you'll be operating either at low risk, as defined in the handbook, or as maybe modified through adaptive management, or you will be operating at a level that's different than low risk, where that decision has been made as a result of a social choice. In other words, [we can] depart from low risk for a defined, in a defined, area by a defined amount for a defined period of time, provided that low risk remains the long-term goal, there's a plan to get to low risk over the long term.

Moreover, some areas are already at high risk because of past logging operations and therefore need to "recruit" old growth over time in order to arrive at low risk. As one First Nations interviewee put it, "to be blunt about it, you've got some ecosystems there that have had so much development in that you're not going to have your old-growth representation that you're looking for 300 years in any case, because you've got to grow it."

The elements of variability, risk, scale, and time serve to render ecology commensurable with economy. Rather than assuming that the two spheres exist a priori and are in inherent conflict with one another, these elements produce new mixtures of people, trees, and animals wherein human activity is viewed as one form of disturbance among many and wherein human disturbance can be inserted at different scales and times given commitments to overall levels of risk. These are specific mechanisms invented by the actors to produce the kind of world that they want – one that includes both ecological integrity and human well-being.

CIII: Rendering Economy Commensurable with Ecology

A second set of procedures was invented to reconcile conservation, development, and justice – this time applied to the sphere of economy to render it commensurable with the sphere of ecology. As mentioned above, during the war in the woods, these two terms were split, pitted against each other in fundamental conflict, and viewed as incommensurable. In contrast, actors involved in the GBR were working to create a hybrid "conservation economy" that consisted of (1) an economy that relied on conservation as its condition of profitability and (2) conservation that provided an economy through the translation of its ecological values into economic values. Moreover, the conservation economy was based on the principle of justice as determined by and designed to benefit those most in need: local First Nations.

The Kit-Git-Pit convened a working group to take the conservation economy from concept to reality. Termed the Conservation Investments and Incentives Initiative (CIII), the group worked to determine the feasibility of the idea. The role and activities of the CIII can be seen in a presentation given by ENGOs to the CCLRMP in 2003 (CIII 2003). The first slide – "CIII Background" – presented the central idea of the conservation economy: while traditionally locked in an inherent zero sum conflict, conservation and economy *can be* viewed as mutually dependent and even positive sum.

CIII Background
- Traditional conflict between conservation and economic development
- Emerging understanding that conservation and local sustainable economies are mutually dependent
- Emerging belief that conservation can be used to attract global investment for use in local economic development
- Emerging interest by many – is this real?
- ENGOs "challenged" by FN, province, and others to demonstrate this is real
- ENGOs propose joint initiative with BC [government] (CIII 2003)

Merely stating that conservation and development are mutually dependent and positive sum does not mean that this is so. There are only an "emerging understanding" and an "emerging interest by many," but we are still left with the question "is this real?" What defines reality? According to Latour (1988, 182), "nothing is by itself either logical or illogical, but not everything is equally convincing. There is only one rule: 'anything goes'; say anything as long as those being talked to are convinced." That is, reality is an achievement that results from processes of "convincing." The first people who needed to be convinced – or who demanded "convince me!" – were First Nations, as one environmentalist indicated:

> The challenge from the First Nations to the enviros ... was ... "put your money where your mouth is." And that's where the seeds of conservation financing [came from] ... So it was a paradigm shift, and it was all a very high-level idea, then we had to get down to the nuts and bolts of "okay, so what does this mean? How are we going to make this real?"

To say that reality is an achievement is not to say that everything is relative and that reality is purely a social construction. The process of convincing is not simply rhetorical: things become real only when they are connected to the "nuts and bolts" that render them strong and durable. But this can only happen through a "challenge" of "demonstration" (or, in Latour's [1987, 87] term, a "trial of strength") through which humans and non-humans are enrolled as allies – or fail to be so enrolled.

Investors were a key ally that the CIII needed to enrol in order to make the conservation economy "real." Once this money was attached to the GBR, it could be used to simultaneously support conservation and development. Another slide from the presentation – "CIII Theory" – put it like this:

CIII Theory
- There are substantial financial resources available globally with interest in investing in conservation
- Some of these resources can be attracted for investment in coastal British Columbia
- These resources can be applied in a manner that leads to locally sustainable economies through new economic development AND supports higher levels of conservation. (CIII 2003)

Who were these theoretical investors with global financial resources? According to the slide, they existed as a network at the intersection of an interest in economic development and an interest in conservation. How this network was formed was not specified by the CIII but said to exist in theory. The primary question, expressed as the "general objective" of the CIII (2003), was this: "Is it possible to exploit the convergence of conservation interests and economic development interests in a way that promotes a legacy of economic health for coastal communities?" Achieving this objective entailed the work of linking money, conservation, jobs, and First Nations. This involved three basic tasks: attracting money, linking money to conservation, and tying conservation money to jobs for First Nations.

Where would the money come from? According to the presentation, there were actors who, given their "convergent" interests, could be enrolled in the network under construction. The work here would consist of identifying "the extent to which conservation-based financial resources exist and are available for investment in BC" as well as "the conditions under which these resources can be attracted to BC" (CIII 2003). Potential investors were identified, including philanthropic groups, the provincial government, the federal government, corporate investors, fund investors, and private individuals. Potential investors were not only identified and differentiated but also aligned with funds that were themselves differentiated into types. Some funds would be tied to conservation management (goal of $60 million), others to economic development (goal of $60 million), and still others to "socially responsible investment."

Links to these funders were made through a conservation financing project engaged in by ENGOs and First Nations operating out of the Kit-Git-Pit.[6] Raising funds to support economic development was a new role for ENGOs, whose focus had traditionally been on protecting wilderness *from* economic development. It thus involved a shift away from the "politics of limits" in which "environmentalists define their interests as limiting human intrusions upon nature" (Nordhaus and Shellenberger

2007, 5). This shift involved some soul-searching by ENGOs, as one environmentalist indicated: "We're going 'should we just tell people they should do it [develop a conservation economy], and now it's their problem, or are we actually going to have to go help find them some money to help, sort of, jump-start that [process]?'"

Building realities is about enrolling allies that, in turn, need to be convinced that they should join the network. ENGOs and First Nations needed to convince funders that the conservation economy was a viable idea and that they should participate in it. In order to do that, other allies were enlisted to translate the idea into terms that would be attractive to potential funders. According to one environmentalist,

> we brought in a very reputed consultant group [Redstone Strategy
> Group] from the US who helped design the conservation financing
> model ... They were sort of working on behalf of a variety of parties,
> including the foundations who didn't want to throw millions of
> dollars at something if it was just basically going to fail.

The consultant collected information from Statistics Canada, First Nations chiefs and council members, regional and provincial economic development officers, business leaders and industry experts, ministry staff, operating companies, NGOs, and interest groups (Redstone Strategy Group 2003). In the process, they visited seven communities in the region, chosen to be representative rather than exhaustive. Consulting the 2001 census, the consultant calculated that the region required 1,750 new jobs (determined by the area population minus non-labour force, employed labour force, and "natural unemployment"). These total jobs were then broken down in an estimated job need by community. Of the 1,750 needed new jobs, the consultant suggested, there was actually a need of only 1,440 new "core" jobs because of the multiplier effect manifested in service sector spinoffs.[7] These jobs were then broken down by sector.[8]

According to one environmentalist, these results were

> a huge piece in our selling the conservation financing ... You go to a
> guy and say, "listen, we are trying to raise $120 million, we're trying to
> raise $60 [million], you're gonna leverage your money – you can
> double your money because we will get the government to put in $60
> [million] – we're going to create economic development and jobs, and
> if we create 200 jobs we will have solved the employment problem in
> this region."

The value of this story in selling conservation financing to funders was even greater given the translations that money would go through to eventually reach conservation. Many of the funders targeted (e.g., the Nature Conservancy) were accustomed to linking money and conservation through the outright purchase of land for the purpose of protection. However, British Columbia's forests are publicly rather than privately owned and for that reason cannot be bought and sold. Thus, in order for funders' money to impact conservation outcomes, it would *first* have to be translated into support for conservation jobs for First Nations, which would *then* be translated into scenarios that specified the specific relationship between funding and land designated for conservation, which would *then* inform First Nations' land-use plans, which would *then* result in a given amount of protection of the land base. According to one environmentalist, this was not an easy thing for funders to "wrap their heads around":

> We had to convince them that, no, we can't buy the land here, we're not buying land to protect it, it's they're going to protect it, but they need an alternative means of economic opportunity, and that's what this is trying to create, those opportunities for them which gives First Nations some, not certainty, but greater confidence in being able to set aside these lands.

Funders were eventually "convinced"; however, enrolment is a two-way street, and funders imposed three sets of conditions on their potential contributions. First, they wanted "legal mechanisms to provide security" (CIII 2003), including assurances that conservation values would be permanently protected and that their protection would be enforced. This involved the legal establishment of a certain amount of protected area (2.25 million hectares). Second, funders required the establishment of "sustainable models of economic development" (CIII 2003) that ensured a high level of employment while protecting the environment and using natural resources prudently. This took the form of establishment and adequate funding of the Ecosystem-Based Management Working Group and an initial suite of legal land-use objectives. And third, funders required that federal funds, which would match the province's $30 million contribution, were in place.

The second major task of the CIII was to link money to conservation. In the zero sum "trees versus jobs" paradigm, more conservation means less money and vice versa. In contrast, the CIII attempted to link these things in positive sum terms. In the words of one environmentalist, the means of linking conservation and development were provided by the mediation of the international community (taking the form of investors interested in conservation):

> If you're [i.e., a First Nation] gonna take an opportunity hit and not log a bunch of stuff in your territory, that means that you are taking some global responsibility, and the world needs to help pay you for the fact that you're taking an opportunity hit and pay for the opportunity cost.

Trees can be translated into employment by cutting them down and linking them to international retailers of forest products. However, the forest can also be translated into employment by linking standing trees to international funders who will pay for the "opportunity cost" of conservation. How was this to play out in practice? According to an ENGO presentation (Rainforest Solutions Project 2003, 3), "through conservation financing, conservation investors make a financial investment in a First Nation based on the conservation value of their LUP [land-use plan]." That is, money was specifically tied to the amount and value of land designated for conservation in First Nations' land-use plans, based on four considerations.

1   The amount of land area in conservation status (i.e. no resource extraction activity)
2   The biodiversity values of the land (biodiversity indices)
3   The contiguous nature of the conservation and restoration areas (clusters)
4   The percentage of a First Nation territory in conservation or restoration toward protection status (5)

In fact, money and land were connected in a specific formula: "50% Conservation Value + 30% Protection Value + 20% Complex Value = Conservation Financing Available to a First Nation" (6). The conservation value was determined by a "protection factor" and a "restoration to protection factor," the latter of which was given half the weight of the former. The percent protection value was determined by the percent of the First Nation's territory in protection, with higher protection giving higher value.

The complex value was "based on the contribution made by watersheds to the creation of larger complexes" (Rainforest Solutions Project 2003, 10), with greater contribution giving higher values. The result was a clear positive link between the amount and value of land put into conservation status and the amount of money that First Nations were eligible to receive.

However, this arrangement was differentiated from market transactions since, as mentioned above, the land in question was not considered a commodity. As made clear in the presentation, "the amount of each proposal in no way reflects the monetary value of the land" since "the real ecological and cultural values of these lands cannot be named in monetary terms." Thus, conservation financing "is not about buying land or buying conservation" (4). Not only was this point important to help potential funders "wrap their heads around" the idea of conservation financing, but it was also important to assuage fears of undue foreign economic influence on domestic policy issues. One environmentalist responded to the idea that

> US funders are controlling what's happening in BC, and it's like ...
> first of all, it's just wrong, you go ask US funders, they did not design
> EBM or any of these things, they were brought in, and a lot of the
> funders that funded stuff were brought in after the fact. You know, the
> criteria and everything had been developed based on the LRMP, and
> so the criteria for the conservation funding dollars to come in are
> what's in the LRMP.

Rather, the purpose was to provide options and incentives for First Nations to conserve their territories. First Nations in the process of developing LUPs were encouraged to put their draft land-use scenarios into the formula in order to inform their final LUPs.

The third task in making the conservation economy real was tying conservation money to jobs for First Nations. As can be seen in the Conservation Investments and Incentives Agreement,[9] this task was split into two parts: tying conservation to jobs and tying jobs to conservation. The first half of this task involved providing mechanisms that would link the designation of land for conservation with employment opportunities for First Nations. In the past, conservation was equated with job loss; in the case of the GBR, the question was how could conservation be tied to job creation? The philanthropic funds provided the mediation. The second half of this task involved the development of businesses that depended, as a condition of their profitability, on conservation. In other words, these would be jobs that ensured rather than undermined sustainability. The kinds of businesses that these funds were intended to support included shellfish aquaculture; fisheries; technology and communication; wildlife viewing; nutriceuticals; mushroom harvesting; non-timber forest products; tourism, including cruises and wildlife viewing; EBM-compliant forestry operations; non-nuclear- and non-carbon-burning energy projects; green building projects; and small-scale, non-toxic, subsurface rock, mineral, or gem extraction projects.

The provincial and federal governments each contributed $30 million toward an economic development fund in support of such businesses. Whether such businesses can in fact be successful remains an open question. Indeed, a great deal of skepticism exists about the ability of the region to invent a conservation economy based on new businesses. Nevertheless, the funds have been put in place, making at least this aspect of the conservation economy – "putting your money where your mouth is" – real. As recounted by one environmentalist, "when that announcement happened this year, I don't know how many chiefs came up to me and said, 'we never believed it, I have to tell you, yes I went to all those meetings, and yes we talked about this, [but] I never believed it would ever happen.'"

In sum, EBM and the conservation economy help to render ecology and economy mutually commensurable. By using the mechanisms of variability, scale, risk, and time, ecological integrity is reworked to make space for human well-being. By tying conservation to money and economic development to conservation in the conservation economy, human well-being is reworked to make it commensurable with ecological integrity. Through these mechanisms, trees, animals, and people will find one good, common world to inhabit. However, "putting in order" refers to more than processes of commensuration: it also means instituting the matter of concern as a matter of fact.

Turning the Matter of Concern into a Matter of Fact

As should be apparent in the foregoing, the procedures developed by the Kit-Git-Pit to reconcile conservation and development also integrated issues of justice for First Nations. Their interests in control and decision making were translated into the very structure of the pilot project. Moreover, the *EBM Handbook* explicitly recognized First Nations' interests while translating them into a project that seeks to reconstitute ecology in order to render it commensurable with economy. On the other hand, First Nations' interests were taken into account in the CIII's efforts to alter economy to become commensurate with ecology.

Additionally, after these processes were fed into the LRMP processes and they had made their final recommendations (Central Coast LRMP Completion Table 2004; North Coast LRMP Planning Table 2004), these recommendations were not forwarded directly to the provincial government for it to make a decision. There were now two forms of government recognized in the province: the provincial government and First Nations governments. First Nations were no longer regarded as one stakeholder among many. Therefore, the recommendations went to a two-year process of "government-to-government negotiations" between the province and individual First Nations. ENGOs and forestry companies supported the elevation of First Nations to the status of government. However, during these negotiations, the entire network – so tenuously stitched together – threatened to break down. The JSP ground to a halt while forestry companies sought to align themselves with First Nations and the province rather than ENGOs. On the other hand, ENGOs were pilloried by their environmental colleagues for squandering the power that they had generated in a substandard deal. Attacked by other environmentalists, their alliances – and thus their strength – weakened. Moreover, the alliances that they had made with industry and First Nations strengthened the project but threatened to shift its focus too far away from ENGOs' goals. According to one environmentalist interviewee,

> as the environmental sector, we're getting shot at from every single quarter because people are basically saying, "look see, you guys basically made an agreement that's not going to stick, trees are coming down, it's all fucked up" … So we're basically losing our social licence to even be in the conversation, as the environmental objective. Industry is basically in a place of "you know what? Maybe we can hide behind First Nations and governments on this, maybe we don't actually need to be in the conversation with you on this anymore because we're not really that scared of you anymore because maybe you don't have a market campaign that can hurt us anymore." … That was our dark night of the soul.

As Callon (1986) reminds us, there is no inevitability to networks. Realities, whether they are knowledges, technologies, or land-use agreements, do not materialize because they are intrinsically true, superior, or good. Moreover, there is no force behind them that brings them into being. Rather, realities are produced through tenuous processes of network formation. Elements are cajoled to enrol in a network; if they defect, then the network will not survive. The "dark night of the soul" for ENGOs arose from the possibility that the matter of concern that they had worked so hard to institute as a matter of fact could so easily fall apart. However, they managed to regroup and commit the industry to certain "milestones" along the way to implementing EBM. Eventually, the agreement was announced on February 7, 2006.

The provincial government called it a "New Vision for Coastal BC" (British Columbia 2006). Of the 6.4 million hectares covered by the agreement, 1.8 million received protected status. The remainder, aside from "biodiversity areas," were open to industrial forestry operations. However, the agreement did not simply segregate ecological protection from industrial exploitation via zoning: under the agreement, the two objectives bled into one another. On the one hand, logging was to operate under EBM. On the other, protected areas did not restrict all types of economic practice. First Nations had a key hand in writing new "conservancy" legislation, ensuring that the establishment of class A parks did not preclude their interests. Along with expected practices such as ecotourism, other opportunities, such as shellfish aquaculture, were permissible. As well, mining and small-scale hydroelectric development were permitted in areas zoned as "biodiversity operating areas."

The agreement attracted international attention. The BC government (2006) told the world that "provincial land use decisions for the Central Coast and the North Coast will preserve some of the most spectacular, ecologically diverse regions in the world." Moreover, these decisions were the result of "an unprecedented collaboration between First Nations, industry, environmentalists, local governments and many other stakeholders." These actors and their "diverse interests have come together in a unique partnership that will support economic opportunity while preserving some of B.C.'s most spectacular wilderness areas and protecting habitat for a number of species." Meanwhile, the announcement cited First Nations representative Dallas Smith, who suggested that the agreement meant that "our people have a more active role in how and where business is done in our traditional territories, and we can move toward cultural, ecological and economic stability in this region." Finally, the province announced that the elements of protection and EBM "demonstrate B.C.'s commitment to sustainable forest practices, something international markets are demanding."

Fragility of the GBR Network

The network of trees, valleys, bears, activists, the public, markets, forestry companies, and First Nations assembled by environmentalists was now an agreement. Its various elements and features were represented and mobilized in a document and an announcement that travelled around the world. Yet it was a shaky network, and controversy remained. As in Callon's (1986) study of the domestication of scallops, dissent is an ever-looming possibility. Callon showed how the network, put together by scientists to support their knowledge of scallops, fell apart once fishermen (who until then had accepted their representation without protest) rejected their role and fished the scallops. The scallops dissented by refusing to anchor. Scientific colleagues dissented by criticizing the scientists' findings. In the case of the GBR, there are also important degrees of dissent from all sides, which might eventually lead to the undoing of the agreement.

Environmentalists' criticism of the RSP has largely to do with fundamental concerns about EBM: the slowness with which it is being implemented, the lack of clarity with which it is understood, and its appropriateness as "compensation" or "safety net" for a lower than desired percentage of protected areas. In the absence of EBM implementation, by some accounts, logging has increased on the central coast to a level "unprecedented in 15 years" (McAllister, as cited in Blunt 2006). According to Lisa Matthaus of Sierra BC, "we are [still] seeing clear-cuts, landslides, the same old stuff. Right now the forest industry has a volume-driven model" (cited in Hume 2006). Part of the reason for the delay in implementing EBM is the complexity of the task. Since EBM has never been implemented on an industrial scale anywhere in the world, no clear models exist to guide implementation. Discussions are still taking place on around what exactly EBM *is* (Sterritt 2007). Finally, and linked with the uncertainty continuing to surround it, there is a concern that EBM is not sufficient to compensate for actual protection. In 2003, the Coast Information Team recommended that 44-60 percent of the GBR be protected from industrial activity. Environmentalists agreed to the lower level proposed, 32 percent, because of the compensation that would be provided by EBM. However, some see this as a risky strategy. As a member of the Raincoast Conservation Society writes, "designating nearly 70% of the most significant expanse of coastal temperate rainforest on earth as a laboratory for an untested experimental forest management regime and calling it a 'safety net' would appear to be an exercise in 'faith-based' conservation" (Genovali 2005).

These concerns threaten to disrupt, halt, or even undo the delicate new world being stitched together in the GBR. As expressed by Simon Jackson (2007) of the Spirit Bear Youth Coalition, "with the agreement coming under increasing fire from those that believe progress has been too slow or simply inexistent, there is growing speculation that the historic agreement may come undone altogether – possibly pushing all parties back to the drawing board yet again." A key criticism is that the RSP, in agreeing to the deal and ceasing its market campaign, gave up both its source of power and the logging moratoriums. As Earth First!er Zoe Blunt (2006) writes,

> it's difficult to sum up the anger and betrayal some BC enviros and First Nations feel about the Great Bear Rainforest agreement. Certainly the Big Greens have squandered a tremendous amount of trust and goodwill. I can't imagine what will happen if they were to come back to the Nuxalk or the Valhalla Wilderness Society and say, as they did when the process started, "We need your help – let's work together. Trust us. We're on the same side; we can all be winners."

Indeed, grassroots groups have been critical of the agreement. The Valhalla Wilderness Society (n.d.) complained that EBM guidelines, originally based on biological research, were so watered down by the government that they are now too weak to ensure protection of wildlife. The organization also complained that the 2009 phase-in was too slow, allowing destructive forestry practices to continue in the interim. As noted above, the Raincoast Conservation Society has also voiced criticism of the deal. As reported by Butler (2006), the "Raincoast [Conservation Society] never liked the process that produced February's agreement. It remained aloof and tried, unsuccessfully, to persuade its environmental allies to do the same. 'They gave up a big card by participating,' says [Ian] McAllister. 'Everything that we predicted has happened.' Additionally, the Spirit Bear Youth Coalition has complained that not enough of the spirit bear's habitat has been protected, resulting in the organization's leader, Simon Jackson, refusing to be present during the 2006 announcement. The coalition criticizes plans to log Green Inlet, an area of the spirit bear's range not protected by the Spirit Bear Conservancy. This stand pits the coalition not only against the province but also against the Kitasoo First Nation, who own the licence to log the area.

Such criticisms affect the "mobilization" moment of translation since they question the RSP's authority to represent the interests of non-human nature and the desires of other environmentalists. The announcement and much press coverage might have presented the agreement as an "unprecedented" achievement of collaboration, but dissent continues to rage. To some small environmental groups, the JSP is an example of corporate environmentalism, an approach that prefers to work behind closed doors with power brokers while ignoring the interests and desires of smaller groups. Given that the environmental movement in British Columbia has largely been consistently local and grassroots (Wilson 1998), the challenges that the RSP faces might not go away.

Moreover, mobilization of the agreement faces challenges from other groups. As described earlier, non-Aboriginal forestry-dependent communities reacted strongly to news that ENGOs and forestry companies were negotiating about resource management on public lands. From the perspective of some non-Aboriginal community members, local workers' interests have not been protected by the CIII agreement and have been ignored in the interests of achieving cooperation from First Nations. The campaign to shut down the alliance (Operation Defend) failed to get off the ground, and some believe that they have been systematically excluded and marginalized throughout the network-building process. This is a significant shift in the relations of power as local, non-Native, forestry-dependent communities, through their spokespeople mayors, once had clout because of their key position in the "compact" between the government and the forestry industry (Wilson 1998). However, their power relative to the other groups has diminished. A mechanism has been designed specifically to enable stakeholder engagement in decision making and implementation of the agreement: the Plan Implementation Committees (PIMCs) made up of the same groups that participated in the LRMPs. However, according to one environmentalist interviewee,

> the PIMCs were specially manufactured by all parties at the governance level to be as ineffective as possible ... Almost no budget, they've got, I'm not going to say these words, I was about to say terrible words. They've got a series of individuals on them who are not the right individuals to be engaged in an innovative, visionary, and creative solution-building conversation about how to implement these decisions. They have, basically, the victims and the folks who are least empowered and least intellectually capable of having conversations that are required. So they basically stacked it up so that it becomes a place where you can just waste a lot of time. You certainly can't effectively engage in any kind of stakeholder decision making or collaboration.

Communities have gone from a position of collaboration to one of consultation in which their memberships are viewed as tokenistic. It is interesting to witness how the provincial Liberal government has abandoned its traditional power base of local resource communities. By dealing with First Nations as governments and by accepting decisions made by a coalition of environmentalists and forestry companies, the Liberals have neglected local communities. There is a touch of irony here since original conservation economy plans included a component specifically designed to take into account the interests of impacted communities. The plan would have included a "socially responsible investment" component that would have been aimed at impacted communities on northern Vancouver Island and elsewhere. However, the Liberal government refused to consider the proposal since it considered it to be too much like a subsidy and a disruption of the operation of free markets. Will local communities return to haunt this agreement? What will happen with a change of government? While it is difficult to see at this point how it would happen, it is possible that dissent from communities could make the GBR fall apart.

Beyond unhappy environmentalists and disenfranchised communities, other excluded parties might come back to haunt the GBR. Not all First Nations, for example, are happy with the agreement. In fact, two First Nations – the Nuxalk and Lax Kw'Alaams – have never signed on. Some people in the forestry industry are also bitter and believe that they got a very bad deal. Individuals in the provincial government have expressed dissatisfaction with the process. Some non-humans have also been left out: for example, some argue that too little information on coastal wolves resulted in inadequate attention to their habitat needs (McAllister 2007). The GBR collective, like any association of humans and non-humans, is fragile, in constant need of renewal, and at risk of falling apart.

Even in February 2006, the agreement remained a "vision." Even more work was required to implement it and make it a reality. Subsequent to government-to-government negotiations, protocols were signed between the province and First Nations committing both to the "full implementation of EBM by March 31, 2009."[10] Just what "full implementation" meant was defined by the new co-governance institution – the Land and Resource Forums – designed to implement the decision. These forums specified a number of conditions to be met in order to consider EBM as fully implemented. First, a "governance framework" would have to be in place. It involved collaborative mechanisms linking First Nations and the province, including the Land and Resource Forums and collaborative management agreements. Additionally, the framework included collaborative mechanisms for stakeholders, including an EBM Working Group and the Plan Implementation and Monitoring Committees.

Second, mechanisms to foster human well-being, or "socioeconomic policies and initiatives that seek to achieve a high level of human well-being over time" (Joint Land and Resource Forums 2007, 1), had to be in place. These mechanisms included institutionalization of the CIII in the Coast Opportunities Fund (made up by the Coast Economic Development Society and the Coast Conservation Endowment Fund Foundation); renewal of the Coast Sustainability Trust (mitigation measures for workers adversely affected by the agreement); regional economic development policies and initiatives; and capacity-building programs.

Third, mechanisms had to be in place to maintain ecological integrity. Such measures would "seek to achieve a low level of ecological risk overall in the Central and North Coast, over time" (Joint Land and Resource Forums 2007, 1). This included land zones, which included protected areas such as conservancies and biodiversity areas; landscape reserves; and specific land-use objectives to guide operations.

Fourth, in recognition that full implementation referred to implementation of a *plan* to achieve ecological integrity and human well-being over time rather than by March 31, 2009, the Land and Resource Forums specified that an "adaptive management" mechanism had to be in place to "support the further development and implementation of EBM beyond 2009" (Joint Land and Resource Forums 2007, 1). This included a system for monitoring and evaluating ecological integrity and human well-being, a data management system, and a decision support and analysis system.

And fifth, the Land and Resource Forums required that implementation would involve "a suite of flexibility tools that can be used to facilitate transition and sustain First Nation and local community well-being" (Joint Land and Resource Forums 2007, 1). These "flexibility tools" included the ability to manage different levels of risk in different watersheds and landscapes. Also required was the ability to conduct operations at different levels of risk, and, for specified periods of time, higher levels of resource development activity would be allowed.

THE GBR COLLECTIVE

All of these conditions were in fact met by March 31, 2009, allowing the government to declare that "the Province has met its commitment to establish an Ecosystem-Based Management (EBM) system for coastal B.C. by March 31, 2009" (British Columbia 2009). In this respect, the matter of concern first articulated by a joint ENGO-forestry company group was turned into a matter of fact. As I described above, the matter of concern took shape when this group established itself as an obligatory point of passage for the network that would form around it. In contrast to the tendency in the modern constitution to separate nature and society (while illicitly associating them), the joint ENGO-forestry industry group launched a project that *explicitly* attempted to mix them together. Thus, the project sought to bring together a variety of human and non-human groups and to articulate their interests. In a further shift away from the modern constitution, one of the groups so designated – First Nations – strongly rejected the idea that experts alone could go out and find the facts with which to bring closure to public debate. The attempt to achieve premature closure through science, as noted in earlier chapters, was an unfortunate tendency that reproduced the modern constitution. In contrast, First Nations argued that all relevant groups should be part of a common research endeavour. Here facts and values, science and politics, also began to mix. The focus was on making sure that the relevant parties were part of research processes so that the questions investigated would be deemed "appropriate."

On this basis, environmentalists, forestry companies, and First Nations set out to articulate their interests via the "occasion" offered by the "proposition" of EBM. The work that went into the *EBM Handbook* helped to define the collective that was to emerge. The process of "taking into account" is ensured by the principles of assessment and collaboration. The process of "putting in order" is effected through mechanisms designed to make commensurate ecology and economy, via EBM, and to make commensurate economy and ecology via the conservation economy. As I have detailed in this section, these new arrangements among people, trees, and animals have been instituted as a (revisable) fact.

As a result, the modern constitution approach to BC wilderness politics has been replaced by the collective. This shift was not produced by something external to the networks themselves – by some social structure or force operating above the action. Rather, the shift resulted from other shifts *within* the networks themselves. The collective is a process, and the process continues through implementation of the plan. This is a complex process involving even more science, even more politics, and even more relations among environmentalists, forestry companies, First Nations, communities, and the provincial government. The EBM Working Group is engaged in projects seeking to determine indicators of human well-being and to define protocols for adaptive management. The Plan Implementation and Monitoring Committees convene meetings and rail against the EBM Working Group for not conducting research "on the ground." The JSP sponsors EBM Learning Forums to inform local communities about this new approach to land (and human) management. First Nations translate their land-use plans into detailed strategic plans. ENGOs engage with First Nations to try to influence the development of those plans. The RSP runs "scenarios" on computer programs to determine how much old growth needs to be retained. The provincial government adjusts its land-use orders on the basis of public input. Individuals move from government positions to environmental groups, from environmental groups to the provincial government, from the provincial government to First Nations groups. Travel journalists write stories about encountering grizzlies in the Great Bear Rainforest. Ian McAllister forms a new environmental organization and writes a new coffee table book, this time about the coastal wolves of the GBR. Money is disbursed to First Nations for conservation research and entrepreneurial green businesses. Critics criticize. But, at some point, one has to accept that, while the network process continues, grows, and changes, the analysis has to stop.

Conclusion

Several years have passed since the GBR agreement was finalized. The announcement has faded into the never-ending media stream, environmentalists have moved on to newer, even more important, campaigns, and First Nations – steadfastly committed to the exercise of Aboriginal rights – remain where they have always been. Readers are now linked to the GBR through the tenuous mediation of this book. They have followed environmentalists on a journey of more than fifteen years along British Columbia's coast (riding along in boats, planes, satellites, databases, and images), within the shifting strategic contours of the BC environmental movement, upon trees-become-commodities travelling to the global market, between myriad interests undergoing mutually induced transformations, and, finally, to a place called the Great Bear Rainforest (contested as it is). What does all this mean, and where might it all go? I offer four possibilities.

First, the GBR demonstrates that environmentalists can dismantle seemingly insurmountable obstacles by treating foes as networks and by intervening at strategic locations. Actors are powerful not because of their favourable position in a determinate social structure or because of social forces that only they have access to. Rather, actors gain power as an effect of networks. Sever one key link in the network, and Goliath will fall to its knees. This position aids environmentalists in their desire to move beyond the valley-by-valley battles of the past. Motivated by the strategy of "blockade and media," past conflicts pitched the "forces" of the media and the public good against the "force" of capitalism in an attempt to coerce the state to "set aside" a few remnants from the status quo (Wilson 1998). Although moderately successful, this approach will never be able to fundamentally transform a system so conceived. In contrast, a network approach digs deeply into the dynamics of power. By tracing the networks constituting oligoptica, environmentalists can focus their energies and develop significant leverage to go for big wins.

Second, this strategy will be effective only if environmentalists take responsibility for the networks in which they have intervened. Environmentalists generally demonstrate a strong tendency to purify the networks in which they intervene, as exhibited repeatedly in the case of the GBR. Their goal is usually to establish nature as a special category in need of protection from society. However, nature so identified is actually a co-production of humans and non-humans, while environmentalists consider only some human practices sufficiently "unnatural" to be banned. Rather than directing their sense of moral duty to "wilderness" alone, environmentalists can extend their responsibility to the entire network comprising the matter of concern that they were instrumental in co-producing. So extended, their concern could focus on carefully *remaking* the networks that they have traced, taken apart, and altered, thereby reconnecting key elements such as grizzlies, First Nations, forestry companies, and forestry workers. Collaboratively remaking nature would avoid the myth of "pristine wilderness," which even some environmental organizations have identified as a problem, while avoiding the corresponding myth that nature is solely socially constructed.

Third, the GBR teaches us that remaking nature involves not only translating elements so reconvened (e.g., grizzlies into umbrella species, First Nations into Coastal First Nations, forestry companies into the Coast Forest Conservation Initiative, etc.) but also allowing ourselves to be similarly transformed. Beginning with the goal of protecting the GBR in one big park, conventionally understood, environmentalists ended up focusing comparable amounts of energy on innovating forestry management practices and co-developing a new regional economic development strategy. In order to succeed in the implementation of a conservation vision, environmentalists eventually have to let go of the vision, let it shift and evolve according to the relational interests of the network convened around it, and contribute to its implementation in its entirety. The process of letting go of control is risky and frightening. Our identities, goals, and objectives become defined in relation to whom and what we are connected, so there might be a strong tendency to draw rigid boundaries to protect cherished values. There might be valid reasons to reject networks in which those values do not comprise a key principle of network formation, as in the LRMP. However, where interests can be merged to create a good common world, its realization will be contingent on a degree of self-transformation. The "love strategy" might be a useful way to avoid defensiveness and to draw out the best parts of all parties involved.

Fourth, remaking nature via reassembly and translation is different from negotiating compromises and trade-offs with respect to a given, biophysical reality (the latter was a key approach of the LRMP). The idea of compromise and trade-off rests on the assumption of fixed identities and interests and the corresponding assumption that ecology and economy are related in a zero sum fashion. In this scenario, any consideration given to economy (as represented by industry) is equated with a loss for ecology; equally, any consideration for ecology (as represented by environmentalists) is taken to be a cost to economy. The innovative feature of the GBR, in contrast, is to render these two "domains" commensurable and relatable in positive sum terms (in principle if not yet in practice). Negotiation, then, does not have to be between rigid (human) interests but a process in which humans and non-humans become articulated into a common matter of concern. Moreover, rather than playing the role of the mutely represented or those that speak truth to power, non-humans can play active roles in negotiation. They are network members in their own right, and their interests and identities are determined through various inquiries (e.g., coarse and fine ecological filtering) and through their reactions to the actions of the network (e.g., EBM forestry practices).

Ultimately, the GBR prompts us to reconsider the metaphysics of conservation. The world is not split into a realm of ephemeral human political interests, on one side, and cold, hard, non-human scientific facts, on the other. Or it is – but only as a consequence of the reproduction of this particular formulation. Environmentalists reproduce this formulation when they seek to protect the last imperilled pieces of "pristine wilderness" from myopic capitalists. Academics reproduce this formulation when they debate whether the nature that environmentalists try to save is real or socially constructed. An alternative formulation renders metaphysics an *achievement:* a tenuous, fraught, contentious, and beautiful process on which lives depend. When the old metaphysics no longer serve, it is time to refashion everything – matter, biology, economy, institutions – to remake the one good common world. *Tracking the Great Bear* is a small contribution in this regard, having composed and materially extended the GBR networks through the mediation of this book and having symbolically repackaged them in an attempt to influence environmentalists and others to take up the task of remaking nature in as informed and careful a manner as possible. The task is now yours to translate this fragile offering into your terms and to extend the best of the GBR network as widely as you see fit.

Notes

FOREWORD

1 See, for examples, G.B. Ingram, M, Gibbons, C. Hatch, R.B. Hatch, T. Berman, and L. Maignon, *Clayoquot and Dissent* (Vancouver: Ronsdale, 1994); R. MacIsaac and A. Champagne, eds., *Clayoquot Mass Trials: Defending the Rainforest* (Gabriola Island: New Society Publishers, 1994).

2 See, for examples, M. McGonigle and W. Wickwire, *Stein: The Way of the River* (Vancouver: Talonbooks, 1988); Islands Protection Society, *Islands at the Edge: Preserving the Queen Charlotte Islands Wilderness* (Vancouver: Douglas and McIntyre, 1984); E. May, *Paradise Won: The Struggle for South Moresby* (Toronto: McClelland and Stewart, 1990).

3 L. Stefanick, "Baby Stumpy and the war in the woods: Competing frames of British Columbia Forests," *BC Studies* 130 (Summer 2001): 41-68; T.J. Barnes and R. Hayter, "The restructuring of British Columbia's coastal forest sector: Flexibility perspectives," *BC Studies* 113 (Spring 1997): 7-33; R. Hayter, "The war in the woods: Post-fordist restructuring, globalization and the contested remapping of British Columbia's forest economy," *Annals of the Association of American Geographers* 93, 3 (2003): 706-29; R. Hayter, *Flexible Crossroads: The Restructuring of British Columbia's Forest Economy* (Vancouver: UBC Press, 2000); C. Harris and J. Barman, "Photoscape: Fordism in the mills," *BC Studies* 113 (Spring 1997): 35-37.

4 N. Bomley, "'Shut the Province Down': First Nations blockades in British Columbia," *BC Studies* 111 (Autumn 1996): 5-35.

5 W. Magnussen and K. Shaw, *A Political Space: Reading the Global through Clayoquot Sound* (Minneapolis: University of Minnesota Press, 2003).

6 J.C. Day, T.I. Gunton, T.M. Frame, K.H. Albert, and K.S. Calbick, "Toward rural sustainability in British Columbia: The role of biodiversity conservation and other factors," in S.S. Light, ed., *The Role of Biodiversity in the Transition to Rural Sustainability* (Amsterdam: IOS Press, 2004), 101-13; G. Hoberg, "The British Columbia Forest Practices Code: Formalization and its effects," in M. Howlett, ed., *Canadian Forest Policy: Adapting to Change* (Toronto: University of Toronto Press, 2001), 348-77.

7 Although the Kitlope Valley, the last undeveloped watershed greater than 100,000 hectares in extent, had been protected in 1994 by agreement between the Haisla First Nation, the provincial government of British Columbia, and the West Fraser Timber Company, which voluntarily relinquished its cutting rights in the area. T. Berman with M. Leiren-Young, *This Crazy Time: Living Our Environmental Challenges* (Toronto: Alfred A. Knopf, Canada, 2011), 128.

8 M.K. Moore and S. Beebe, *Coastal Watersheds: An Inventory of Watersheds in the Coastal Temperate Forests of British Columbia*, A BC Endangered Spaces Project Working Paper, Earthlife Canada Foundation; Ecotrust/Conservation International (1991). See also *Coastal Temperate Rain Forests: Ecological Characteristics, Status and Distribution Worldwide*, Ecotrust and Conservation International (1992), available at http://archive.ecotrust.org/publications/ctrf.html.

9 *The Rain Forests of Home: An Atlas of People and Place,* originally published by Ecotrust, Pacific GIS, and Conservation International (1995), available at http://www.inforain.org/rainforestatlas/index.html.

10 *The Rain Forests of Home*, 6.

11 The eight million hectares figure and the complex ecosytems quote are from Ecotrust Canada, *North of Caution: A Journey through the Conservation Economy on the Northwest Coast of British Columbia* (Vancouver: Ecotrust Canada, 2001), 1; the "accelerated pace" fear is attributed to P. McAllister in R.A. Rajala, *Up-Coast: Forests and Industry on British Columbia's North Coast, 1870-2005* (Victoria: Royal BC Museum, 2006), 223; on charismatic megafauna, see F. Ducarme, G.M. Luque, and F. Courchamp, "What are 'charismatic species' for conservation biologists?," *BioSciences Master Reviews* 1(July 2013): 1-8, available at http://biologie.ens-lyon.fr/biologie/ressources/bibliographies/pdf/m1-11-12-biosci-reviews-ducarme-f-2c-m.pdf?lang=en; J. Wilson, *Talk and Log: Wilderness Politics in British Columbia* (Vancouver: UBC Press, 1998).

12 These developments are discussed in several places. See Berman, *This Crazy Time*, 128-40, and Rajala, *Up-Coast*, 224.

13 Zirnhelt and Clark, quoted in Rajala, *Up-Coast*, 224.

14 The "forest to the people" and "acre every sixty seconds" quotes are from Berman, *Crazy Time*, 135.

15 A cost of $200 million in lost contracts is suggested by D. Riddell, "Case study III: Evolving approaches to conservation – integral ecology and Canada's Great Bear Rainforest," in S. Esbjörn-Hargens and M. Zimmerman, eds., *Integral Ecology: Uniting Multiple Perspectives on the Natural World* (Boston and London: Integral Books, 2009), 454-75. See also D. Riddell, "Evolving approaches to conservation: Integral ecology and Canada's Great Bear Rainforest," *World Futures* 61, 1 and 2 (2005), 63-78.

16 Rajala, *Up-Coast*, 226

17 M. Smith and A. Sterritt, with P. Armstrong, "From conflict to collaboration: The story of the Great Bear Rainforest," 12, available at http://sfigreenwash.org/downloads/WWFpaper.pdf.

18 The "Great People Rain Forest" argument is made by I. Gill, "Canada's forgotten coast," in Ecotrust Canada, *North of Caution*, 3.

19 Rajala, *Up-Coast*, 226.

20 Premier Ujjal Dosanjh, quoted in Rajala, *Up-Country*, 227. See also L. Davis, "Home or global treasure? Understanding relationships between the Heiltsuk Nation and environ-

mentalists," *BC Studies* 171 (Autumn 2011), 9-36, and M. Low and K. Shaw, "Indigenous rights and environmental governance: Lessons from the Great Bear Rainforest," *BC Studies* 172 (Winter 2011/2012): 9-33.

21 In this general vein, see R.A. Clapp and C. Mortenson, "Adversarial science: Conflict resolution and scientific review in British Columbia's Central Coast," *Society & Natural Resources* 24 (2011): 902-18.

22 More details on the EBM prescribed for the area can be found in Smith and Sterritt, "From conflict to collaboration," 8-9, and in the EBM Handbook and EBM Framework at http://www.citbc.org.

23 O. Tjornbo, F. Westley, and D. Riddell (Social Innovation Generation@University of Waterloo), *Case Study: The Great Bear Rainforest Story* (January 2010), available at http://sig.uwaterloo.ca/highlight/case-study-the-great-bear-rainforest-story.

24 J. Law, "After ANT: Complexity, naming and topology," and B. Latour, "On recalling ANT," both in J. Hassard and J. Law, eds., *Actor-Network Theory and After* (Oxford: Blackwell Publishers 1999), 7 and 19, respectively. For an account of the difficulties in explaining ANT, see the exchange between a professor and a student in B. Latour, *Reassembling the Social: An Introduction to Actor-Network Theory* (New York: Oxford University Press, 2005), 141-59.

25 N. Bingham, "Actor-network theory (ANT)," in D Gregory, R. Johnston, G. Pratt, M.J. Watts, and S. Whatmore, eds., *The Dictionary of Human Geography* (Chichester: Wiley-Blackwell, 2009), 6-7. The sensibility claim is here attributed to John Law; the following discussion also draws upon Bingham's summary.

26 For other engagements of Latour with the Great Bear Rainforest, see J. Dempsey, "The politics of nature in BC's Great Bear Rainforest," *Geoforum* 42, (2011): 211-21; J. Dempsey, "The birth of the Great Bear Rainforest: Conservation science and environmental politics on British Columbia's central and north coast," MA Thesis, Department of Geography, University of British Columbia, 2006; and, in part, J. Whittet, "Wild nature, disciplined aesthetics: Framing environmental justice in the case of the Northern Gateway Pipeline project," MA Thesis, McGill University, 2012.

27 The basic definition of networks is that adopted by R. Lejano, M. Ingram, and H. Ingram, *The Power of Narrative in Environmental Networks* (Cambridge, MA: MIT Press, 2013), 5.

28 J. Law and M. Callon, "Engineering and sociology in a military aircraft project: A network analysis of technological change," *Social Problems* 35, 3 (1988): 285.

29 Lejano, Ingram, and Ingram, *The Power of Narrative*, 3.

30 For a somewhat differently framed account, see R.A. Clapp, "Wilderness ethics and political ecology: Remapping the Great Bear Rainforest," *Political Geography* 23 (2004): 839-62.

31 Quoted in Lejano, Ingram, and Ingram, *The Power of Narrative*, 38.

32 Berman (*Crazy Time*, 129) claims to have helped come up with the Great Bear Rainforest name during discussions over dinner in San Francisco with Valerie Langer, Karen Mahon, and Ian McAllister in 1995 or 1996, but Peter McAllister says he was using the term at least a couple of years earlier (Richard Mackie, private communication, 8 May 2014). The "storytellers" phrase is from Berman, *Crazy Time*, 39.

33 Berman, *Crazy Time*, 39.

34 Lejano, Ingram, and Ingram, *The Power of Narrative*, 174.

35 Ibid., 173.

Introduction

1 Unless otherwise noted, all details about interviewees, except for the groups to which they belong, are confidential.

Chapter 1: Where in the World Is the Great Bear?

1 Here I focus on the McAllisters' photos and stories rather than on their mobilization of science, since I dealt with science more fully in the preceding sections and since this is the main focus of the authors themselves: "We have tried to include the basic information required to understand this vast and complex area, but our main purpose has been to express our own appreciation of it" (16).
2 Or "historicity" in Latour's (1999, 149-50) terms. Latour uses this term to contrast the notion of history associated with a correspondence theory of truth – in which facts, if they exist, have always been there, outside history, while history is reserved for humans – with a recognition of the history of things – involving a series of transformations constituting circulating reference.
3 I refer to these entities with the prefix *quasi* because they are the provisional results of networks made up of humans and non-humans.
4 I discuss the concept of proposition more fully in Chapter 3 in connection with ecosystem-based management.

Chapter 2: Grizzlies Growl at the International Market

1 This blockade built on earlier protests against logging in the area that began in 1995 when the Nuxalk House of Smayusta invited environmentalists to join forces with it. On September 3, 1995, Nuxalk hereditary chiefs and community members were joined by Forest Action Network (FAN) at their blockade at Ista (Frog Creek) (where members of FAN hung a banner reading "Interfor Stop Clearcutting the Great Coast Forest – Forest Action Network"). By September 12, sixty people were at the site, comprised of Nuxalk (hereditary chiefs, elders, band council members, and community members) and FAN activists, later joined by three Heiltsuk hereditary chiefs. On September 26, RCMP officers confronted the forty or so people remaining at the blockade. Twenty-two people were arrested, including three hereditary chiefs and five FAN activists.

Chapter 3: Negotiating with the Enemy

1 Individual negotiations between ENGOs and forestry companies had already begun. In February 1998, Interfor negotiated with ENGOs, agreeing to defer logging in several operating areas and to test variable retention logging at one site in return for ENGOs' participation in the LRMP and their agreement not to oppose activities in three less con-tentious areas. While an agreement was reached in July 1998, a similar agreement with Western Forest Products took longer to achieve. By March 1999, the Sierra Club of BC and Greenpeace had agreed to participate in the LRMP.
2 ENGOs party to the agreement included Coastal Rainforest Coalition, Rainforest Action Network, Natural Resources Defense Council, Greenpeace International, Greenpeace Canada, and Sierra Club of British Columbia. Forestry companies that were party to the

agreement included Canadian Forest Products, Fletcher Challenge Canada, International Forest Products, West Fraser Timber, Western Forest Products, and Weyerhaeuser.

3 The Letter of Intent went through several drafts, with the final, unsigned draft dated March 31, 2000. It is difficult to say which changes were made to the draft after a March 2 version was leaked to the media around March 15, but many of the main elements were in place as confirmed by details reported in news stories on March 16 (Hamilton 2000; Hume 2000; Lee 2000).

4 The breakdown of the number of valleys by company is as follows: Interfor, 25; West Fraser, 20; Western Forest Products, 28; Weyerhaeuser, 5. Twenty-two valleys were also included in the standstill that were not allocated to any company at the time. The total number of included valleys was 104.

5 However, neither forestry companies nor ENGOs gave up everything. On the one hand, ENGOs were able to maintain their overall "ancient forests" campaign, so long as they did not specifically target the companies party to the agreement vis-à-vis their geographical areas of operation (coastal British Columbia). On the other, forestry companies required that ENGOs not protest their operations in less contentious areas.

6 Environmentalist Tzeporah Berman in an interview on CBC's *The National*, June 16, 1999.

7 Their anger contained a degree of irony since these groups helped to establish the joint ENGO-CFCI group in the first place when, in 1998, they asked ENGOs and forestry companies to negotiate and resolve their disputes over logging moratoriums because of concerns that the LRMP was making little headway and would be deemed illegitimate without the participation of ENGOs. However, they did not know that their request about moratoriums would be translated into a project to radically restructure land use and management.

8 The campaign requested millions of dollars in funding from the provincial government, but the request was not granted, and the campaign never got off the ground.

9 At the David Suzuki Foundation, which provided funding.

10 In June 2000, eight coastal First Nations signed the Declaration of First Nations of the North Pacific Coast (Turning Point 2000), committing them to work together to address the above issues. The First Nations were Council of the Haida Nation (Old Massett and Skidegate Councils), Gitga'at Nation (Hartley Bay), Haisla Nation (Kitamaat Village), Heiltsuk Nation (Bella Bella), Kitasoo/Xaixais Nation (Klemtu), and Metlakatla Nation.

11 The Met refers to the Metropolitan Hotel in Vancouver where they took place. There were both small meetings among ENGOs, forestry companies, and First Nations, larger meetings among those groups in addition to labour and communities, and side meetings. The provincial government sent a representative to observe the meetings but was not invited to participate.

12 Supported by a $10 million fund provided by the government, later increased to $35 million by the newly elected Liberal government.

13 General Protocol Agreement on Land Use Planning and Interim Measures between First Nations and the Government of British Columbia, 2001 (http://www.coastforest conservationinitiative.com/pdf/finalprotocol.pdf).

Chapter 4: Mobilizing Allies and Reconciling Interests

1 Latour (2004, 83) plays with the meaning of the term "proposition" to indicate how matters of concern are uncertain, tied both to language and to reality (since the world is "loaded" into discourse), and involve a "new and unforeseen association."

2 Latour (2004, 86) also plays with the meaning of the word *articulation* to make a theoretical point. He writes that, if something is articulated, it is so "in every sense of the word: that it 'speaks' more, that it is subtler and more astute, that it includes more articles, discrete units, or concerned parties, that it mixes them together with greater degrees of freedom, that it deploys longer lists of actions."

3 Another method of representing the trees and animals of the coastal region is through representative species, including umbrella, keystone, and indicator species. While such species have been identified for the region (grizzly bears, salmon, and northern goshawks respectively), and while they have been recommended by the CIT as suitable representatives, the CIT made specific recommendations only with respect to representative ecosystems.

4 More specifically, representative ecosystems are determined in relation to an ecosystem classification system developed in British Columbia termed the biogeoclimatic ecosystem classification system (Pojar, Klinka, and Meidinger 1987). This system uses "site series" to indicate general ecological types on the basis of differences in climate, topography, and soil. Each site series or group of site series defines a particular ecosystem, the protected portion of which will "represent" the ecosystem type and thereby the plants, trees, and animals that are typical constituents thereof.

5 These figures were controversial but withstood a trial of strength in the form of a risk threshold workshop (Price, Holt, and Kremsater 2007).

6 Although the idea of the conservation economy was originally adopted by ENGOs given their interest in justice and the plight of First Nations, it was even more forcefully engaged with by First Nations when they took an active role in developing it – so much so that it came to be seen, at least from their perspective, as their idea.

7 Note the symmetry between the CAD, which worked to define "core conservation areas," and Redstone, which worked to define "core jobs" for the region.

8 With 430 going to shellfish aquaculture and fisheries, 460 going to cruise ship and high-end lodge tourism, 275 going to sustainable forestry and non-timber forest products (mushroom harvesting), 85 going to conservation activities, and 190 going to "other."

9 Conservation Investments and Incentives Agreement, 2007, between the Coast Conservation Endowment Fund Foundation; the Coast Economic Development Society; and the Nature Conservancy, William and Flora Hewlett Foundation, Gordon and Betty Moore Foundation, David and Lucile Packard Foundation, the Rockefeller Brothers Fund, and Tides Canada Foundation. Available at http://www.coastfunds.ca/system/files/07-05-02%20 Conservation%20Investments%20and%20Incentives%20Agreement%20-%20Signed%20 -%20FINAL.pdf.

10 Land Use Planning Agreement-in-Principle between Coastal First Nations and the Government of British Columbia, 2006 (available at http://archive.ilmb.gov.bc.ca/slrp/lrmp/ nanaimo/central_north_coast/docs/Turning_Point_Protocol_Agreement_Signed.pdf), and between the KNT First Nations and Government of British Columbia, 2006 (http:// www.nanwakolas.com/sites/default/files/AIP%20FInal%20Signed%20Version.pdf).

References

Aikman, H., B. Beese, L. Brown, D. Cardinall, D. Crockford, G. Fraser, et al. 2004. *Ecosystem-Based Management Framework*. Vancouver: Coast Information Team.

Amsterdamska, O. 1990. Surely you are joking, Monsieur Latour! *Science Technology and Human Values* 15, 4: 495-504.

Beebe, S., and E. Wolf. 1991. The coastal temperate rain forest: An ecosystem management perspective. In *Coastal Watersheds: An Inventory of Watersheds in the Coastal Temperate Forests of British Columbia,* edited by K. Moore. Vancouver: Earthlife Canada Foundation and Ecotrust/Conservation International.

Berman, T. 2006a. Behind the scenes at the Great Bear agreement. ForestEthics. http://www.forestethics.org/.

–. 2006b. Speech to Bioneers. Paper presented at the 17th Annual Bioneers Conference. ForestEthics. http://www.forestethics.org/.

–. 2011. *This Crazy Time: Living Our Environmental Challenge*. Toronto: Knopf Canada.

Besel, R.D. 2011. Opening the "black box" of climate change science: Actor-network theory and rhetorical practice in scientific controversies. *Southern Communication Journal* 76, 2: 120-36. doi: 10.1080/10417941003642403.

Bled, A.J. 2010. Technological choices in international environmental negotiations: An actor-network analysis. *Business and Society* 49, 4: 570. doi: 10.1177/0007650309360705.

Blok, A. 2010a. Divided socio-natures: Essays on the co-construction of science, society, and the global environment. PhD thesis, Department of Sociology, University of Copenhagen. http://www.dasts.dk/wp-content/uploads/Anders-Blok-2010.pdf.

–. 2010b. War of the whales: Post-sovereign science and agonistic cosmopolitics in Japanese-global whaling assemblages. *Science, Technology and Human Values* 36, 1: 55-81. doi: 10.1177/0162243910366133.

Bloor, D. 1999a. Anti-Latour. *Studies in History and Philosophy of Science* 30, 1: 81-112.

–. 1999b. Discussion: Reply to Bruno Latour. *Studies in History and Philosophy of Science* 30, 1: 131-36.

Blunt, Z. 2006. Great Bear Rainforest: The clearcut truth. Gorilla News Network. http://
zoeblunt.gnn.tv/.

Braun, B. 2002. *The Intemperate Rainforest: Nature, Culture, and Power on Canada's West
Coast.* Minneapolis: University of Minnesota Press.

Braun, B., and N. Castree. 1998. *Remaking Reality: Nature at the Millennium.* London:
Routledge.

British Columbia. 1996. Backgrounder: Land and resource management plans. Integrated
Land Management Bureau, Ministry of Forests, Lands, and Natural Resource Operations.
http://www.ilmb.gov.bc.ca/.

–. 2006. Province announces a new vision for coastal B.C. News release, Ministry of Agriculture and Lands. http://www2.news.gov.bc.ca/news_releases_2005-2009/2006AL0002
-000066.htm.

–. 2009. EBM protects coastal jobs, culture, and environment. News release, Ministry of
Agriculture and Lands. http://www2.news.gov.bc.ca/news_releases_2005-2009/2009AL
0007-000588.htm.

Brundtland, G.H. 1987. *Our Common Future: The World Commission on Environment and
Development.* Oxford: World Commission on Environment and Development.

Burningham, K., and G. Cooper. 1999. Being constructive: Social constructionism and
the environment. *Sociology: The Journal of the British Sociological Association* 33, 2:
297-316.

Butler, D. 2006. War in the woods: The Great Bear Rainforest sellout. *Ottawa Citizen,* 26
November, B5.

Callon, M. 1980. Struggles and negotiations to define what is problematic and what is not:
The sociology of translation. In *The Social Process of Scientific Investigation: Sociology of
the Sciences,* edited by K. Knorr and R. Whitley, 197-219. Boston: Reidel.

–. 1986. Some elements of a sociology of translation: Domestication of the scallops
and the fishermen of St. Brieuc Bay. In *Power, Action, and Belief: A New Sociology of
Knowledge?,* edited by J. Law, 196-229. Boston: Routledge and Kegan Paul.

Callon, M., and B. Latour. 1981. Unscrewing the big Leviathan: How actors macrostruc-
ture reality and how sociologists help them to do so. In *Advances in Social Theory and
Methodology: Toward an Integration of Micro- and Macro-Sociologies,* edited by K.D.
Knorr-Cetina and A.V. Cicourel, 277-303. Boston: Routledge and Kegan Paul.

Callon, M., and J. Law. 1982. On interests and their transformation: Enrolment and
counter-enrolment. *Social Studies of Science* 12, 4: 615-25.

Canadian Broadcasting Corporation. 1997. The fight over "Spirit Bear." *The National,* 26
May.

Canadian Rainforest Network. 1998. The Great Bear Rainforest conservation toolkit. http://
www.fanweb.org/resources/reports.html.

Cardinal, D. 2004. *Ecosystem-Based Management Planning Handbook.* Vancouver: Coast
Information Team.

Cashore, B.W. 2001. *In Search of Sustainability: British Columbia Forest Policy in the 1990s.*
Vancouver: UBC Press.

Castree, N., and B. Braun. 2001. *Social Nature: Theory, Practice, and Politics.* Malden, MA:
Blackwell Publishers.

Catton, W.R., and R.E. Dunlap. 1978. Environmental sociology: New paradigm. *American
Sociologist* 13, 1: 41-49.

Central Coast Land Resource Management Plan. 2001. *CCLRMP Phase 1 Framework
Agreement.* Vancouver: CCLRMP.

Central Coast LRMP Completion Table. 2004. *Report of Consensus Recommendations to the Provincial Government and First Nations.* Vancouver: CCLRMP.

Clapp, R. 2004. Wilderness ethics and political ecology: Remapping the Great Bear Rainforest. *Political Geography* 23, 7: 839-62. doi: 10.1016/j.polgeo.2004.05.012. http://linkinghub.elsevier.com/retrieve/pii/S096262980400068X.

Coady, L. 2002. Dynamics of change: The BC forest sector case example. Paper presented at the New Terms of Engagement for Global Leaders Conference, 4 April.

Coady, L., and M. Smith. 2003. *The Pathway to Resolving the Dispute over the "Great Bear Rainforest": New Approaches to Land Use Planning and Conservation in Ecologically Important Forests on the BC coast.* Vancouver: Joint Solutions Project.

Coast Forest Conservation Initiative. 2001. Coastal forest companies believe major breakthrough on forest and environmental issues is at hand. Media release, 19 February. http://www.coastforestconservationinitiative.com/pdf2/CFCImajorbreakthroughfeb01.pdf.

Conroy, M. 2007. *Branded! How the "Certification Revolution" Is Transforming Global Corporations.* Gabriola Island, BC: New Society Publishers.

Conservation Investments and Incentives Initiative (CIII). 2003. Identifying the conditions for conservation-based investment. Presentation prepared for the CCLRMP, Vancouver.

Cronon, W. 1996. The trouble with wilderness: Or, getting back to the wrong nature. In *Uncommon Ground: Rethinking the Human Place in Nature,* edited by W. Cronon, 69-90. New York: W.W. Norton.

Cullen, D., G.J.A. McGee, T. Gunton, and J.C. Day. 2010. Collaborative planning in complex stakeholder environments: An evaluation of a two-tiered collaborative planning model. *Society and Natural Resources* 23, 4: 332-50. doi: 10.1080/08941920903002552.

Curtis, M. 1997a. Boycott campaign targets B.C. goods. *Times-Colonist,* 11 June.

–. 1997b. Greenpeace blockades logging site. *Times-Colonist,* 22 May.

–. 1997c. Natives urge Greenpeace to stop protest. *Times-Colonist,* 28 May.

–. 1997d. Watered-down protest: Crew thwarts protesters with high-pressure. *Times-Colonist,* 22 August.

Davis, L. 2009. The high stakes of protecting Indigenous homelands: Coastal First Nations' turning point initiative and environmental groups on the B.C. West Coast. *International Journal of Canadian Studies* 39-40: 137-59.

Dempsey, J. 2011. The politics of nature in British Columbia's Great Bear Rainforest. *Geoforum* 42, 2: 211-21. doi: 10.1016/j.geoforum.2010.12.003.

Derworiz, C. 1999. Bus brings rainforest issues to urbanites. *Calgary Herald,* 1 August, A11.

Dovetail Consulting. 2000a. *Summary Report: CED Scoping Session for the Central and North Coast.* Vancouver: ENGO-CFCI Steering Committee.

–. 2000b. *Summary Report: Socio-Economic Workshop for the Central and North Coast of B.C.* Vancouver: Joint Solutions Project.

–. 2000c. *Workshop Summary: Technical Consultation on an Ecosystem-Based Planning Framework for the Central and North Coast of British Columbia.* Vancouver: ENGO-CFCI Steering Committee.

Doyle, A., B. Elliott, and D. Tindall. 2000. Framing the forests: Corporations, the BC Forest Alliance, and the media. In *Organizing Dissent: Contemporary Social Movements in Theory and Practice,* edited by W. Carroll, 240-68. Toronto: Garamond Press.

Dunlap, R.E., and W.R. Catton Jr. 1994. Struggling with human exemptionalism: The rise, decline, and revitalization of environmental sociology. *American Sociologist* 25, 1: 5-30.

Econews. 1996. The Canadian rainforest network. *Econews Newsletter,* April, 49.

Eden, S. 2009. The work of environmental governance networks: Traceability, credibility and certification by the Forest Stewardship Council. *Geoforum* 40, 3: 383-94. doi: 10.1016/j.geoforum.2008.01.001.

Findlay, A. 2007. The Great Bear market. *BC Business Online,* 1 October. http://www.bcbusinessonline.ca/node/1345.

Fong, P., and A. McCabe. 1998. Greenpeace launches British offensive against BC logging: As the province's timber industry reels from the Asian flu, the environmental group condemns logging in what it calls BC's "Great Bear Rainforest" in a calculated effort to hurt lumber sales. *Vancouver Sun,* 3 March, A1.

Frame, T., T. Gunton, and J.C. Day. 2004. The role of collaboration in environmental management: An evaluation of land and resource planning in British Columbia. *Journal of Environmental Planning and Management* 47, 1: 59-82. doi: 10.1080/0964056042000189808.

Fuller, S. 2007. *New Frontiers in Science and Technology Studies.* Cambridge: Polity Press.

Genovali, C. 2005. Cutting the bears out of the Great Bear Rainforest. *Counterpunch,* 28 September. http://www.unz.org/Pub/CounterpunchWeb-2005sep-00237.

Gigg, R. 2006. The Great Bear Rainforest: The power of naming. *Courier-Islander,* 10 March, A13.

Globe and Mail. 1998. BC logging protests staged in Europe: Greenpeace occupies embassy roof in Bonn, *Globe and Mail.* 6 April, A12.

Greenpeace. 1997a. BC log barge occupied to protest rainforest destruction. http://archive.greenpeace.org/.

–. 1997b. BC lumber ship heading for Europe marked as rainforest destroyer. http://archive.greenpeace.org/.

–. 1997c. Great Bear Rainforest: The facts. http://archive.greenpeace.org/.

–. 1998a. Greenpeace blockades ship from entering Long Beach. http://archive.greenpeace.org/.

–. 1998b. Rainforest destruction: Environmentalists protest against pulp freighter from Canada. http://archive.greenpeace.org/.

–. 1998c. US and European corporations turn away from BC rainforest wood. http://archive.greenpeace.org/.

–. 1999. *The Chain of Destruction: From Canada's Ancient Rainforests to the United States Market.* Washington, DC: Greenpeace. http://www.greenpeace.org/usa/Global/usa/report/2010/2/the-chain-of-destruction-fro.pdf.

Greenpeace and Sierra Legal Defense Fund. 1997. *Broken Promises: The Truth about What's Happening to British Columbia's Forests.* Washington, DC: Greenpeace.

Hall, N. 1997. Greenpeace fights blockade injunction: Logging protest splits Nuxulk Indians. *Vancouver Sun,* 10 June, B4.

Hamilton, G. 1996. Clear-cut fight: Behind-scenes campaign building for several years to shift focus north. *Vancouver Sun,* 4 June, C1.

–. 2000. Logging-environmental negotiations break down: Groups excluded from process – primarily Native Indians – force delay in initiative. *Vancouver Sun,* 30 May, D1.

–. 2006. Vast area of new parks ends coastal controversy. *Vancouver Sun,* 8 February, D1.

Hannigan, J.A. 2006. *Environmental Sociology.* 2nd ed. New York: Routledge.

Hayter, R. 2000. *Flexible Crossroads: The Restructuring of British Columbia's Forest Economy.* Vancouver: UBC Press.

–. 2003. "The war in the woods": Post-Fordist restructuring, globalization, and the contested remapping of British Columbia's forest economy. *Annals of the Association of American Geographers* 93, 3: 706-29.

Holifield, R. 2009. Actor-network theory as a critical approach to environmental justice: A case against synthesis with urban political ecology. *Antipode* 41, 4: 637-58. doi: 10.1111/j.1467-8330.2009.00692.x.

Holt, R., A. MacKinnon, J. Pojar, K. Price, and L. Kremsater. 2004. *Scientific Basis of Ecosystem-Based Management.* Vancouver: Coast Information Team.

Howlett, M., J. Rayner, and C. Tollefson. 2009. Forest policy and economics from government to governance in forest planning? Lessons from the case of the British Columbia Great Bear Rainforest initiative. *Forest Policy and Economics* 11: 383-91. doi: 10.1016/j.forpol.2009.01.003.

Hume, M. 2000. Secret deal would halt logging in coastal B.C.: Union predicts outrage: Environmentalists, industry have plan to end costly boycott. *National Post,* 16 March, A2.

–. 2006. A victory in the fight to preserve B.C.'s rainforest. *Globe and Mail,* 7 February, S1.

Hunter, J. 1997. Forest protests promised: Premier Glen Clark says Greenpeace campaigners are enemies of B.C. *Vancouver Sun,* 26 April, B6.

Irwin, A. 2001. *Sociology and the Environment: A Critical Introduction to Society, Nature, and Knowledge.* Malden, MA: Polity Press.

Jackson, S. 2007. Earth Day update: Spirit Bear's future still uncertain. Spirit Bear Youth Coalition. http://www.spiritbearyouth.org/?p=299.

Jackson, T., and J. Curry. 2004. Peace in the woods: Sustainability and the democratization of land use planning and resource management on Crown lands in British Columbia. *International Planning Studies* 9, 1: 27-42. doi: 10.1080/1356347042000234961.

Jeo, R.M., M.A. Sanjayan, and D. Sizemore. 1999. *A Conservation Area Design for the Central Coast Region of British Columbia, Canada.* Salt Lake City: Round River Conservation Studies.

Jepson, P., K. Buckingham, and M. Barua. 2011. What is a conservation actor? *Conservation and Society* 9, 3: 229. doi: 10.4103/0972-4923.86993.

Joint Land and Resource Forums. 2007. Full implementation of ecosystem based management "EBM" by March 31, 2009. http://archive.ilmb.gov.bc.ca/slrp/lrmp/nanaimo/central_north_coast/docs/Full_Implementation_%28Final%20July%202010%202007%29.pdf.

Joint Solutions Project. 2000. Letter of intent. 31 March. http://web.uvic.ca/.

Jolivet, E., and E. Heiskanen. 2010. Blowing against the wind: An exploratory application of actor network theory to the analysis of local controversies and participation processes in wind energy. *Energy Policy* 38, 11: 6746-54. doi: 10.1016/j.enpol.2010.06.044.

Kranjc, A. 2002. Conservation biologists, civic science, and the preservation of BC forests. *Journal of Canadian Studies* 37, 3: 219-38.

Krauss, C. 2006. Canada to shield 5 million forest acres. *New York Times,* 7 February. http://www.nytimes.com/2006/02/07/international/americas/07canada.html?pagewanted=all&_r=0.

Landström, C., S.J. Whatmore, S.N. Lane, N. Odoni, N. Ward, and S. Bradley. 2011. Coproducing flood risk knowledge: Redistributing expertise in critical "participatory modelling." *Environment and Planning A* 43, 7: 1617-33. doi: 10.1068/a43482.

Latour, B. 1987. *Science in Action: How to Follow Scientists and Engineers through Society.* Cambridge, MA: Harvard University Press.

–. 1988. *The Pasteurization of France.* Cambridge, MA: Harvard University Press.

–. 1991. Technology is society made durable. In *A Sociology of Monsters: Essays on Power, Technology, and Domination,* edited by J. Law, 103-31. London: Routledge.

–. 1993. *We Have Never Been Modern.* Trans. C. Porter. Cambridge, MA: Harvard University Press.

–. 1999a. *Pandora's Hope: Essays on the Reality of Science Studies.* Cambridge, MA: Harvard University Press.

–. 1999b. For David Bloor ... and beyond: A reply to David Bloor's "Anti-Latour." *Studies in History and Philosophy of Science* 30, 1: 113-29.

–. 2004. *Politics of Nature: How to Bring the Sciences into Democracy.* Trans. C. Porter. Cambridge, MA: Harvard University Press.

–. 2005a. From realpolitik to dingpolitik or how to make things public. In *Making Things Public: Atmospheres of Democracy,* edited by B. Latour and P. Weibel, 14-43. Cambridge, MA: MIT Press.

–. 2005b. *Reassembling the Social: An Introduction to Actor-Network Theory.* New York: Oxford University Press.

–. 2007. A plea for earthly sciences. Paper presented at the Annual Meeting of the British Sociological Association, 12-14 April.

Law, J. 1986. On the methods of long-distance control: Vessels, navigation, and the Portuguese route to India. In *Power, Action, and Belief: A New Sociology of Knowledge?,* edited by J. Law, 234-63. London: Routledge and Kegan Paul.

–. 2008. Actor network theory and material semiotics. In *The New Blackwell Companion to Social Theory,* 3rd ed., edited by B.S. Turner, 141-58. Oxford: Blackwell.

Leader-Williams, N., and H.T. Dublin. 2000. Charismatic megafauna as "flagship species." *Conservation Biology* 3: 53-84.

Lee, K. 2000. Activists and loggers close to rainforest truce: Boycott campaign end linked to protection of trees in disputed area. *Times-Colonist,* 16 March, A1.

Lee, N., and S. Brown. 1994. Otherness and the actor network: The undiscovered continent. *American Behavioral Scientist* 37, 6: 772-90.

Lien, M.E., and J. Law. 2011. "Emergent aliens": On salmon, nature, and their enactment. *Ethnos 76,* 1: 65-87. doi: 10.1080/00141844.2010.549946.

Lockie, S. 2007. Deliberation and actor-networks : The "practical" implications of social theory for the assessment of large dams and other interventions. *Society and Natural Resources* 20, 9: 785-99. doi: 10.1080/08941920701460317.

Low, M., and K. Shaw. 2011. First Nations rights and environmental governance: Lessons from the Great Bear Rainforest. *BC Studies* 172: 9-34.

Luke, P. 1996. Coast not clear: Eco-groups, foresters face off over logging. *Province,* 6 August, A23.

MacLennan, D. 2000. Forest minister defends NDP's land use plan. *Courier-Islander,* 30 May, A1.

Marchak, P. 1983. *Green Gold: The Forest Industry in British Columbia.* Vancouver: UBC Press.

Markey, S., J.T. Pierce, K. Vodden, and M. Roseland. 2005. *Second Growth: Community Economic Development in Rural British Columbia.* Vancouver: UBC Press.

Matas, R. 1997. BC hemlock faces boycott: British furniture maker will make switch to pine to protest West Coast logging practices. *Globe and Mail,* 14 November, A7.

McAllister, I. 2007. *The Last of the Wild Wolves: Ghosts of the Great Bear Rainforest.* Vancouver: Greystone.

McAllister, I., and K. McAllister. 1997. *The Great Bear Rainforest: Canada's Forgotten Coast.* Madeira Park, BC: Harbour Publishing.

McCrory, W. 2003. A personal view from the Spirit Bear campaign co-ordinator. http://www.savespiritbear.org/.

McGee, G., A. Cullen, and T. Gunton. 2010. A new model for sustainable development: A case study of the Great Bear Rainforest regional plan. *Environment, Development and Sustainablility* 12: 745-62. doi: 10.1007/s10668-009-9222-3.

McLintock, B. 1997. Greenpeace halts clear-cut. *Province,* 22 May, A7.

Moore, K. 1991. *Coastal Watersheds: An Inventory of Watersheds in the Coastal Temperate Forests of British Columbia.* Vancouver: Earthlife Canada and Ecotrust/Conservation International.

Murphy, R. 1994. The sociological construction of science without nature. *Sociology: The Journal of the British Sociological Association* 28, 4: 957-74.

Newmark, W.D. 1995. Extinction of mammal populations in western North American national parks. *Conservation Biology* 9, 3: 512-26.

Nordhaus, T., and M. Shellenberger. 2007. *Break Through: From the Death of Environmentalism to the Politics of Possibility.* Boston: Houghton Mifflin.

North Coast LRMP Planning Table. 2004. *North Coast Land and Resource Management Plan: Final Recommendations.* Vancouver: North Coast LRMP.

Pemberton, K. 1998. Greenpeace blocks BC ship: Activists climb crane of vessel to halt unloading of timber in Scottish port. *Vancouver Sun,* 27 March, A1.

Pojar, J., K. Klinka, and D. Meidinger. 1987. Biogeoclimatic ecosystem classification. *Forest Ecology and Management* 22: 119-54.

Price, K., R. Holt, and L. Kremsater. 2007. Representative forest targets: Informing threshold refinement with science. Review paper written for RSP and CFCI. http://archive.ilmb.gov.bc.ca/slrp/lrmp/nanaimo/cencoast/docs/representation_paper_posted.pdf.

Rainforest Solutions Project. N.d. Great Bear Rainforest backgrounder. http://www.savethegreatbear.org/.

–. 2003. Conservation financing for First Nations. Presentation prepared for North Coast LRMP. Vancouver: Rainforest Solutions Project.

Rayner, J., and P. Zittoun. 2008. Policy by design: The elusive link between problems and policies. Paper prepared for the Annual Meetings of the Canadian Political Science Association, University of British Columbia, 4-6 June.

Redclift, M., and G. Woodgate, eds., 2010. *The International Handbook of Environmental Sociology.* 2nd ed. Northampton, MA: Edward Elgar.

Redstone Strategy Group. 2003. *Coastal BC Economic Development: Phase Two Final Report, Part 1.* Report prepared for CIII.

Rodger, K., S. Moore, and D. Newsome. 2009. Wildlife tourism, science and actor network theory. *Annals of Tourism Research* 36, 4: 645-66. doi: 10.1016/j.annals.2009.06.001.

Rodríguez-Giralt, I. 2011. Social movements as actor-networks: Prospects for a symmetrical approach to Doñana's environmentalist protests. *Prospects* 56: 13-35.

Rossiter, D. 2004. The nature of protest: Constructing the spaces of British Columbia's rainforests. *Cultural Geographies* 11, 2: 139-64.

Sandilands, C. 2002. Between the local and the global: Clayoquot Sound and simulacral politics. In *A Political Space: Reading the Global through Clayoquot Sound,* edited by W. Magnusson and K. Shaw, 139-67. Montreal: McGill-Queen's University Press.

Shaw, K. 2004. The global/local politics of the Great Bear Rainforest. *Environmental Politics* 13, 2: 373-92. doi: 10.1080/0964401042000209621.

Sierra Club, CRC, and Rainforest Action Network. 2001. Environmental groups affirm their commitment to the "rainforest solutions" process. Press release. http://www.coast forestconservationinitiative.com/pdf3/envirocttmtorspoct00.pdf.

Sierra Club of BC. 2006. Canada's rainforest: Worth saving. Victoria: Sierra Club of BC.

–. 2008. Great Bear campaign history. http://www.sierraclub.bc.ca/our-work/gbr/great -bear-campaign-history.

Smith, M. 2006. Great Bear Rainforest Agreement announcement. http://www.mediaroom. gov.bc.ca//DisplayEventDetails.aspx?eventId=36.

Sodero, S. 2011. Policy in motion: Reassembling carbon pricing policy development in the personal transport sector in British Columbia. *Journal of Transport Geography* 19, 6: 1474-81. doi: 10.1016/j.jtrangeo.2011.09.001.

Stansbury, W.T. 2000. Environmental groups and the international conflict over the forests of British Columbia, 1990-2000. Burnaby and Vancouver: SFU-UBC Centre for the Study of Government and Business.

Star, S.L. 1991. Power, technology, and the phenomenology of conventions: On being allergic to onions. In *A Sociology of Monsters: Essays on Power, Technology, and Domination,* edited by J. Law, 25-56. London: Routledge.

Stefanick, L. 2001. Baby stumpy and the war in the woods: Competing frames of British Columbia forests. *BC Studies* 130: 41-68.

Sterritt, A. 2007. Untitled presentation delivered at Our Common Ground symposium, Vancouver, 8 May.

Struck, D. 2006. Huge Canadian park is born of compromise. *Washington Post,* 7 February. http://www.washingtonpost.com/wpdyn/content/article/2006/02/06/AR2006 020601834.html.

Stueck, W. 2000. Charges loom after protest at B.C. sawmill. *Globe and Mail,* 6 September, A2.

Thomas, J., and V. Langer. 1998. Great Bear Rainforest conservation toolkit. Canadian Rainforest Network. http://www.savethegreatbear.org/.

Thoms, C.A. 2011. Co-constructing community forests in Nepal: Mutual constraint in a transnational aid network. *Journal of Natural Resources Policy Research* 3, 3: 303-14. doi: 10.1080/19390459.2011.591750.

Turning Point. 2000. Declaration of First Nations of the north Pacific coast. Paper presented at Turning Point II conference. http://coastalfirstnations.ca/sites/default/files/imce/ Turning_Point_Declaration.pdf.

Union of BC Municipalities Task Force on Coast Forest Conservation Initiative. 2000. *Task Force Report on the Coast Forest Conservation Initiative CFCI.* Vancouver: Union of British Columbia Mayors. http://www.ubcm.ca/.

Valhalla Wilderness Society. N.d. Science information: What scientists say about the Spirit Bear. http://www.savespiritbear.org/.

Weigand, J., A. Mitchell, and D. Morgan. 1992. *Coastal Temperate Rain Forests: Ecological Characteristics, Status, and Distribution Worldwide.* Portland: Ecotrust and Conservation International.

–. 2006. Founders of Spirit Bear proposal applaud protection. http://www.vws.org/.

Western Canada Wilderness Committee. 1992. *British Columbia's Temperate Rainforest.* Vancouver: WCWC.

–. 2000. WCWC pickets outside "Operation Defend" meeting at the Richmond Executive Inn beginning at 7:30 AM, Friday, September 22. News advisory. https://wilderness committee.org/resources/archives/media/release.

Whatmore, S.J. 2009. Mapping knowledge controversies: Science, democracy and the redistribution of expertise. *Progress in Human Geography* 33, 5: 587-98. doi: 10.1177/0309132509339841.

White, D.F., and C. Wilbert. 2009. *Technonatures: Environments, Technologies, Spaces, and Places in the Twenty-First Century.* Waterloo, ON: Wilfrid Laurier University Press.

Willems-Braun, B. 1997. Buried epistemologies: The politics of nature in (post)colonial British Columbia. *Annals of the Association of American Geographers* 87, 1: 3-31.

Wilson, J. 1998. *Talk and Log: Wilderness Politics in British Columbia.* Vancouver: UBC Press.

Winner, L. 1993. Upon opening the black box and finding it empty: Social constructivism and the philosophy of technology. *Science, Technology and Human Values* 18, 3: 362-78.

Index

actor-network theory: action-at-a-distance, 57, 63, 66; actor-networks, 10, 41; assemblage, 9, 10, 23, 41, 57; black box, 35; circulating reference, 26-27, 40; common world, 51, 90, 95, 112, 125; composition of, 46, 95, 103; collective, 14, 23, 38, 42, 68, 84, 90, 92, 118, 119, 120; criticism of, 11, 13; description of, 10-12; enrolment, ch. 3, 11, 25, 44, 50, 69, 71, 84, 86, 91-93, 106-8, 114; and environmental issues, analysis of, 11; explicitation, 60, 64, 71; hybrids, 9, 24, 25, 39, 42, 51, 53, 76, 77, 95, 105; immutable mobiles, 37, 41; interessement, ch. 2, 45, 64, 71; matter of concern, 69-94, 97, 112, 114, 120, 124, 125; mobilization, ch. 4, 8, 25, 38, 54, 67, 95, 97, 115, 116, 117; modern constitution, 42, 51, 60, 66-67, 68, 75, 76, 84, 90, 92, 120; non-humans as actors, 16, 51-53, 57, 100, 125; obligatory point of passage, 69-70, 74, 77-78, 87, 94, 120; oligopticon, 64, 124; panorama, 22, 38, 41-42, 44, 45, 58, 97; problematization, ch. 1, 23, 83; proposition, 42, 98, 99, 120; quasi-object, 41; quasi-subject, 41; symmetry, principle of, 13, 35, 101

Callon, Michel, 10, 13, 23, 32, 35, 45, 51, 52, 54, 69, 83, 95, 113, 115
conflict: in BC's "war in the woods," 6, 9, 21, 27-28, 37, 71-72, 85, 113; and direct action, 54, 55-59, 87; within the environmental movement, 81, 113, 115-17; within First Nations, 118; between First Nations and environmentalists, 56-57, 84, 85-86, 118; between forestry workers and environmentalists, 84, 85, 117-18; between government and environmentalists, 84, 85; and information campaigns, 54-55; and logging blockades, 55-59; and market campaigns, 59-67
conservation economy, 5, 6, 16, 82, 83, 105-12, 118

dualisms: agency and structure, 16, 49, 64, 120, 123; conservation and development, 9, 28, 76, 96, 101; discourse and matter, 11, 23, 28, 36; economy and ecology, 60, 66, 72, 74, 76, 95, 96, 102-12, 125; epistemology and ontology, 11, 26; facts and meanings, 32; facts and values, 90, 92, 120; form and matter, 24, 26-27; local and global, 29, 30, 31, 57-58, 64; natural science and social science, 9;

NATURE|HISTORY|SOCIETY

Printed and bound in Canada by Friesens

Set in Garamond by Artegraphica Design Co. Ltd.

Copy editor: Dallas Harrison

Cartographer: Eric Leinberger